Now Let Me Find
A Stopping Place

A decade of poems, letters and journals

2008-2018

by
Ethan Renoe

Cover Consulting by Kailey Sullivan
www.kaileysullivan.com

Cover Design and Handwriting by Ethan Renoe

For Rack & Rubb

Forever we will have matching tattoos on our calves
and perpetually be asked why we have Spongebob there.
And forever we will have to explain that it's not Spongebob,
it's Doodlebob.

You two are my Dying Bees,
my Cheetah Girls,
my Y.

You're good, good.

I love you very very very very very very very much,
and I'm 94% sure you exist.

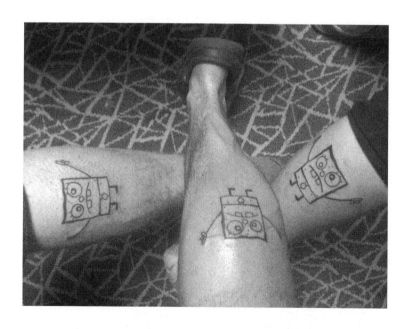

CONTENTS

INTRODUCTION

May 2, 2018

Well, I've done it.

At least, I have done the lion share of the toilsome, un-fun portion of crafting this book. One minute ago I closed a leather bound notebook from 2008 (and a fraction of 2009) in victorious relief. In the past month or two, I have pored over thousands of poems written throughout my life. I'm nearly certain I've read every poem I've ever written.

Now, before you go and get impressed by the *quantity* of poems I've burped up in my lifetime, something needs to be said for their *quality*. Sure, there was the occasional flash of high school brilliance which would surprise me every couple (hundred) pages, but for the most part, my poetry has been a reincarnation of the sad or mushy songs I listened to as a teen. Most of the poems and songs on those pages deserve to go up in flames before anyone else can cast eyes on them.

Spending so much time in the past has been painful in two ways. I once heard an aging rockstar in an interview say something like, "You ever want to torture me, just make me listen to our earliest records."

Reading through so many of my old notebooks has been an amalgam of me cringing, shaking my head, and saying, 'Ohhh, buddy!' the way you simultaneously compliment and discourage a kid scribbling on the walls with crayons.

For your sake, dear reader, I'm glad I underwent the work of eliminating the vast majority of those poems so no one else will have to suffer under them the way I have, though there is an obvious evolution in the quality, topics and tone of the writing.

At the same time, following the path of my life for the past decade via these writings has been painful in the feelings they've revived in me. Not per the raw power of my teenage words or the force of their structure, but in the way they have reminded me of past insecurities and painful events; things that have molded me and pushed my life in *this* direction or *that* one. I've remembered exactly how many times I've been smashed by a painful rejection, or longed for the love of my crush to be reciprocated.

I'll tell you something else I discovered about myself along the way:

A year ago I was having dinner with a married friend of mine. He's twelve years my senior and has three children, but we're alike in many ways. He told me that one of the greatest things about being married is that he can finally, with security and without reserve, lavish his unfiltered love upon his wife.

"We'll be lying in bed and I can express to her the depth of my love without fear that it will be unfounded or that she will leave and that emotion will have been wasted. I can fully tell her how much I love her, and it's safe."

The thing I realized, after wading my way through thousands of these love poems, is that I have wasted a lot of emotion. I have spent it on people who either did not reciprocate my affection, or who simply ended up not working out for one reason or another. If I could go back and chat with Ethan Circa 2008, I would tell him not to squander so much energy on these brief flings.

Save it up.

Wait till you're married.

Spend your energy on other things.

2

Pursue the invisible.

Learn about the world.

It is not hard to see how much of my writing was influenced by romantic comedies and bad music; that the idea of a romantic relationship (though rarely materialized) was a monstrous god throughout my life. And if it seems like I've kissed a million girls, I haven't. Very few, actually. What actually happened is I'd have one kiss and pen twenty poems about it.

And as I have grown in the past decade, I have seen another sort of growth come about, which you may notice as well: A theological maturity. My education for the past 7 years has been mostly biblical and theological, so my view and understanding of God and Scripture has morphed exponentially. And this is something I noticed in many older poems which were attempting to be theological. Once more, I cringed and thought *Really? That's what I thought God was like? That's what I thought Christians were supposed to be like?*

So that is to say, just because I may have included an old poem which makes mention of God doesn't mean it's necessarily what I still believe. Just as (hopefully) you don't believe everything you did 10 years ago! Not that I've fully 'arrived' and have an omniscient understanding of the Holy, but I know a little more than I used to…

& & &

So, what *is* this book?

This book is the result of what I just described: A culling of the better writings of mine from the past ten years. No specific theme, save to examine the ebb and flow of life over a decade with a fledgling writer.

In addition to being a collection of writings I've deemed worthy, this book will be part memoir, as you'll walk through the past ten years of my life, primarily from an internal perspective. These poems, journals and letters express things which were happening on the inside of me more than the outside. For this reason, you'll find brief overviews of the years at the beginning of each chapter, to help contextualize a little bit of which events, people, and places surrounded the creation of each poem. Hopefully they help fit the pieces into the larger tapestry of Ethan's life.

I have also included several posts from my LiveJournal, an early social blogging platform, and a few from my current blog, which I thought helped give context for some of the poems from those eras. They are minimally edited and often embarrassing, and denoted by their bold-fonted titles.

& & &

In regard to the book's title, it came to me as I was writing a poem a few months ago. That poem appears toward the end of this book (3/26/2018) and as I was writing it, it struck me that it's the perfect title for a book of this nature (or for my entire life). As you'll see, I've moved around a *lot*. More than most people. You could say that I've been looking for a stopping place for quite some time.

"Now let me find a stopping place" is also what you may say to your mother or spouse when they call you to supper and you're in the middle of something, and I like that. When you're aware of it, life is an ongoing project, and if you don't find a decent stopping place every now and then, you'll miss the whole thing.

I also chose it to be the title for a poetic book because it's four perfect iambs; a note that only poetry nerds will appreciate.

An art history teacher once told me not to spend more than two hours in any art museum, because beyond that point, you stop absorbing the power of the pieces. They become flat. I think the same is true of this book: It's not meant to be dashed through in huge chunks, but rather slowly digested and appreciated. You won't win an award for reading this book fastest.

Poetry skirts the outer perimeter of human language, and I invite you to walk that boundary with me.

I cited Hemingway in my first book, *Leaving Weather*, though it seems much more fitting here in my fourth: "There is nothing to writing. All you do is sit down at a typewriter and bleed." So without further ado, here is the blood of my last decade of life.

e

2008

SECOND MOVE

I lived on Cape Cod for almost 5 years.

I think that because I wasn't born on Cape Cod, but rather 'came of age' there, I have a golden, sepia-tinted view of my time there. It's a great place to spend puberty. Many who were born there left the Cape with a bitter taste of it in their mouths, while I look back on my time there with an adolescent fondness to which I long to return.

In 2003, I was going into 7th grade when, as the natives say, my family washed ashore. Initially, I hated the Cape, but over the 5 years we were there, I came to love it. At the tail end of 2007, I was dating a girl and loving the bays, marshes and forests of the beautiful peninsula. And that's when my father announced at dinner that we would be returning to Colorado, where I was born.

I was distraught. My middle and high school years had been lived on the Cape, and now the love of my life was here (Well, technically, at boarding school on Long Island but still). Much of 2008 was spent in a state of ambivalent flux, as I returned 'home,' and was around familiar faces and names, but my soul seemed to long for the Cape. My emotions, as a 16-year-old, were confused because I had spent the first half of my time on the Cape longing to be back in Colorado and now I was, and now I didn't want to be.

The second half of 11th grade, I was an outsider again. I had to forge an identity, and opted to be the kid who was moody and mysterious, listening to obscure music no one else knew and writing a lot (Enneagram number 4). It was this year I resolved to write at least one poem a night.

When March came, I had decided to sever the ties with the girl I was seeing due to the distance. A year later, on a late summer stroll on the Cape, she would tell me she was pregnant by her new boyfriend at the age of 17.

At school, my 'new kid popularity' warranted me the title of Prom Prince and later, I'd win Class Clown, but these superficial titles did nothing to abate the deep-seated pain and loneliness I felt on the inside. I can't help but think that this isolation is what led to my idolization of romantic relationships: *If I could just find that* one *girl who would* get *me, then everything would be alright.*

I was trapped in the tension of engaging my new Colorado friends and holding onto my daydreams of Cape Cod.

The brightest ray of hope this year was my best friend Dave. I've known him ever since he stole my due date (June 17, 1991), so I returned the favor and stole his (June 19, 1991). My family moved into a home about a mile from his, so we spent ample amounts of time together. We started a band. We had bonfires in his back yard, accompanied by deep talks and future dreams. We ran and worked out a lot.

Dave is my 27-years-and-counting friend, and I'm grateful for him...

my first post
Feb. 1st, 2008 at 4:54 PM

Since this is my first post, I should start it out with something along the lines of "Ok, this is my first post and I really don't know what to say," but I do know what to say and I'm not sure how much of it exactly I do want to say.

I'm Ethan and I recently heard that our generation is the first to predictably make less than their parents. I can totally see how that prediction could be true. I want more in my life than to merely be a consumer—I want to be a creator. I can't stand it when someone else is making things for me to absorb and take in. I've grown away from watching movies and playing video games toward writing letters and drawing and painting. Right now I am madly in love with a girl whom the angels named Anna, and the only problem is that we are over 2,000 miles away from each other.

I set the mood of this post as apathetic because I just moved here and it's hard for me to care about people here when I am so desperately close to my friends on Cape Cod (which is in Massachusetts, not California).

- **Current Mood:** Apathetic

2/12/2008 aa

Static drips from the
speakers of the radio
as sunflowers dance above
my bed.
This truly is nothing more
than a cardboard box
for a teenage boy
instead.

Beloved, is it nothing but
miles keeping us apart—
no distractions or
cold hands?
I'm holding you down
so you don't fly away, for
I have nothing to say but I love you,
understand?

(next page)

I looked at the clouds
today, hoping they'd bloom.
Now I dance to your music
alone in my room

If I question movement,
I am a stone
but if I question complacency,
am I a hypocrite?

The Secret to Being Me
2/15/2008

Don't be like
anyone else

2/23/2008 aa

I hear a violin
Matt's got a car
so let's pile in

I love you, I just
wish I could show you

3/8/2008

Love is not
what you read,
see or touch.
It's what you
feel when your
heart aches too much

3/14/2008 aa

I'm dead in this distance
inside of your heart
and if you wanted to walk here,
then you'd better start.
I've been sidestepping beauty
like the summer does fall.
These lapping waves recede
like the hope in your calls.
Forgotten chalk-clapped erasers
wiped away my lesson
on putting back the pieces
into the right position.
My fingers are bleeding
like the sky when it rains
from writing you love songs
I couldn't contain.
The new March is coming
but I'm still down here wondering
if last summer's memories
were our glue and it's crumbling.

3/16/2008 aa

So this is it:
the cliff we saw from afar
and here I sit
a cold plastic figure without a heart.

3/20/2008 aa

I miss you at night
when I'm ready for bed,
although sometimes I see you
but just in my head.

My journal's left open
to the page where I wrote
'I love you, I love you'
and that's a direct quote.

But I don't think I meant it,
didn't mean what I said,
so I went out and danced,
put someone in your stead.

Yet I miss you right now
sitting all by myself
wishing you were here
and not anyone else.

Undated notecard, Spring 2008

What you seek
you'll surely find
so you're better off
with it off your mind.

3/20/2008 aa

I saw a scary film tonight
and wished that you were there.
Then everything would feel alright
with you and me both scared.
We would have held each other tight
because we make a real good pair.
I saw a scary film tonight
but someone else was there.

3/22/2008 aa

It is finished,
all the trust I had in you
is all diminished,
cast into the ocean blue.

How could he do that
and why would you let him?
It's now just a fact
our love was interim.

The sun hid today.
In fact, it snowed
and to my dismay,
I just let you go.

You say we're still friends
and yes, I agree.
That will never end—
at least to a degree.

4/15/2008 ak

I settled into my room
inside our new home,
a temporary womb
that I can't call my own
because I can only
stay here so long,
but this love that you've shown me
could prove me wrong.
Will the dust ever settle
like a blanket of tacks?
Said the pot to the kettle:
'My whole home's painted black,'
I moved in my belongings,
put up posters and prints.
I unpacked my things
and fell asleep to the wind.

4/16/2008 ak

I didn't see you tonight,
not unlike I had planned.
It didn't feel right.
I missed you some, and,
if I was a lightbulb
and you were a fuse,
plug us both in
and we'll light up a room.

4/23/2008

Do I thirst for you?
This seed is new,
it was just planted.
Now I'm returning
empty-handed.

When I'm in a crowd
and you're looking at me,
your mind's around
inconsistently.
Like cotton candy.
Slower than leaf changes,
this is taking ages.
I don't love you.
I don't love you.
I don't love you.
I don't love you.
I don't love you.
I don't love you

yet.

5/5/2008

It's a change,
a tidal wave,
so sudden
and sullen
that I really
don't like.
This is my life,
I have just one.
Before I die,
I'd like to be done
living
my
life.

6/6/2008

I'm taking a test
just to see if I'll pass,
if I am good enough
for that mid-middle class.
My future on the line
in the hands of machines
and I have to ask why
all my teachers are mean.
They take down my numbers,
my A's, B's and C's,
but cannot remember
my name or say please.
I am a digit,
a mark on a wall
and I wonder why is it
that I'm here at all.

6/11/2008

I'm calling you tonight—
or tomorrow I should say—
a little after midnight
when the night becomes day.
Pretty soon I'll call you
or leave my voice on your machine
to just say 'What is new?'
or 'Hey, how have you been?'

8/5/2008

It's that changing time again,
when summer turns to fall
and my wardrobe gets longer
and then you start to call.
I feel like a river,
winding, eroding and fluid.
You needed to move
but I went and beat you to it.
Say goodbye to me now
because I don't know who I'll be
come next summer where,
for the first time, we will meet.

8/22/2008

Before the cameras
poisoned the mountains
and drank deeply
from the scars of nature,
a beauty was
created, so perfect
and gentle
that a mere glance
may prove catastrophic.
So through years
and after recovery,
we've accepted a photo
as replacement
beauty.

9/13/2008

I've lost a tree,
said the forest,
or a needle
from the pine.
It wept and wept
from so minuscule
a loss.
Why lose sleep
or even toss
over a wayward
component?

I ask this of
a Shepherd
I love.

The Sun
9/20/2008

When the sun visits
you again, I'll be awake
and longing to be
the sun.

9/24/2008

I'd hate to be
a clearance shelf
where everyone picks
and sorts
all my merchandise,
leaving me messy
as Christmas morning.
Nobody bothers
to organize
the clearance shelf.

9/27/2008

I emptily stare
while you blankly reply
that things have dulled
down between you and I.

My eyes open onto
a blank wall: your words.
Surely you soon must
let me have a turn.

When I Die
9/28/2008

Bury me naked
with an open casket funeral.
Nothing is private in death.

I loved everyone
so very much, much more
than I probably expressed.

Bury me with my blankie
and Fluffy and some art
because I loved all those things best.

And in case it gets cold
so deep in the ground,
throw in a scarf or maybe a vest.

So remember, when I die,
don't put it on me, just beside
because I'd rather not be dressed.

failure

Oct. 18th, 2008 at 10:40 PM

Last night we were going to tp Kendall's house because we drove by and they weren't home. So we went to the 24 hour King Sooper's and got 4 packs of 4 toilet paper rolls and went back to Kendall's house and the whole family had come home. So we went up and rang to doorbell and talked to them for a while about how we were going to tp them but then they came home.

On a side note, if any of you need any extra toilet paper, I have twelve rolls in the Subaru.

college

Oct. 21st, 2008 at 8:45 AM

So I've decided I really like writing and as far as college goes, I'm thinking of now double majoring in English and Art, instead of only art. I like poetry and maybe I'll start a story or something. It's like gravel being rubbed on my ear drums when someone says "I'm doing good."

But now I have to go because study hall is over.

11/25/2008

If I could
accurately describe
a Colorado sunset,
I would be a
millionaire.

11/29/2008

Love is an old lady
and her husband
luggage shopping at
the department store.

> Oh, this is nice, Honey!
> Is it big enough?
> Oh yes, but it's mighty heavy.

They are too weak to lift it,
but they hold one another
gentle like feathers.

> Do you want it?
> Let's check Wal-Mart.
> We already checked Wal-Mart.
> Okay, let's get it.

12/27/2008

I wrote a nice line,
I wrote a good verse
as I wait for my ride
in that ol' tye-dye hearse.

It's an image that's struck me
since I was a boy
who was riding around
in a big Chevy toy.

I've been lying to me
about lying to you
because I'm not so sure
that our dreams will come true.

So write a good line
and pen a nice verse
because soon we will ride
in that ol' tye-dye hearse.

2009

CHASING A GIRL ACROSS AMERICA

I had to be forced to attend my high school graduation.

My attitude was worse than my Beatles hair, and at some point in the spring of 2009, I had decided to move back to Cape Cod for my first year of college. Now, the main reason for this move was a girl from my high school who still lived there, whom I had begun talking with at the time.

I graduated after burning a good number of bridges at my school and headed back to the Cape in June. Of course, when you're gone for a year and a half, people's lives move on without you. I discovered this the hard way as I found that my community had morphed and I didn't quite fit in as well as I once had.

Outsider feeling #93,021.

I dated the girl I had been corresponding with and kissed her on the Fourth of July when we got lost in the woods. It was horrible. It was my first *real* kiss and I froze up like a pufferfish and didn't know whether to keep my eyes open or closed. She told me it was creepy and weird either way and we didn't do it again. That same night, I found out that she went fishing alone with another guy 'just as friends' and I was in distress. I called things off about a month after arriving back in Massachusetts, after dreaming about this girl the entire spring semester.

Not long after that, I lost another dear girl who had been with me for about 13 years: Our family's black Labrador, Dakota. My parents instructed me to drive to a friend's house, where they called me and told me the news. I remember sobbing on the phone as my parents held the phone to Dakota's ear so I could say my distant goodbyes to her. Her eyes had turned yellow and she stopped eating. Later, my dad would say that was one of the worst days of his life. It was the last time I would cry for about four years. Years later, a church service on human trafficking would break that streak and now I choke up whenever I think too hard about the gospel.

Like a freakin' wimp.

In the fall, one of my roommates, Jason, had become increasingly annoyed with my persistently chipper attitude and asked me to move out. A family from church had asked me to housesit for them, so for some reason, I decided to take everything I owned over to their home.

"Why are you taking all this stuff?" the depressed roommate asked. "You're just gonna move it back next week." I shrugged and continued loading up my Jetta.

Three days later, I got a text from the other roommate: "Jason just burnt down the apartment building trying to make fried Oreos." They had lost everything; I lost my mattress.

I ended up moving in with my boss, the owner of a local house painting company. That didn't last long, as I went out for a long run one day and was suddenly hit with the urgent need to go #2. I was about half a mile out from his house on my way back and had to start waddle-running. I made it halfway up his long dirt driveway before my muscles couldn't clench any longer and released.

#2 ran down my legs and into my shoes.

In a frenzied state of panic, I bolted into his house and up the stairs to the bathroom, leaving Ethan-droppings in my wake all over his home.

So *then* I moved in with a lovely elderly French woman named Arlette who baked me croissants and the occasional bowl of ratatouille. She couldn't go up the stairs of her mansion (minutes away from homes owned by Taylor Swift and Arnold Schwarzenegger) so I had it all to myself. Situated feet from beaches, bays and inlets in Hyannisport, it was a runner's dream and I took full advantage of it.

That season was an aesthetically beautiful but lonely existence…

1/28/2009
(On the first page of a notebook)

The first page
always has a poem
about itself.

———

<u>Haiku</u>
The first poem does
always have a poem 'bout
its own existence.

———

And if an epic should
be born in the pages to follow,
let it be deep and strong;
old trees are not hollow.

———

I would love to go home,
feel the warmth of a kiss.
If only I knew
where my home really is.

1/29/2009

So this is the night
that you tell me your fears
of past summer night strolls
and the trees with their tears.
You said there's something about the coast
you can't quite explain,
a humid simplicity
that I lost with a plane.
So I fly to my home
just a few times a year,
but for now I'll walk with you
and lend you my ear.

1/30/2009

Now I sit alone
and I sleep alone.
I drive alone
to shop alone.
I write alone
and I read alone.
I draw alone
and dance alone

etc.

Superbowl
2/1/2009

Just let me say it,
so you can hear it expressed:
I cannot believe that
I missed work for this.
There's a group of boys yelling
and cursing the glass,
while another one's blood
is spread over the grass.
The knuckles and blood
and the awkward positions
don't matter at all to
the fan's superstitions.
So cheer from the crowd,
or the sofa at home,
because a party's a party
when someone's alone.

Let Not Love Come Between Us
2/3/2009

Let not love come between us
as we go about our day to day,
when we drive beneath the darker clouds
and enter in the fray.

Let not love come between us
when I see your face in trees
and ask the simple question:
Who is the Least of These?

Let not love come between us
in the suburbs of Denver,
falling through my bed
in my weakest endeavor.

Let not love come between us
in the dark days of May
when the loving is lost
and my fingers are gray.

2/6/2009
(After being ditched at a school dance)

I'm going alone,
I'm not going with you
and I'm okay with that
if you're alone too.

Your eyes had once burned me
and I was on fire
and I did not know it,
but you're kind of a liar.

We danced in the car
to some foreign new beats,
yet your heart was as cold
as the snow on the street.

2/10/2009

You say
We can be cruel,
we can rip you apart;
we'll cut out your eyes
and we'll slice out your heart.
We'll dance all around
and then keep shouting 'more'
while I lay there ignored,
face down on the floor.
It's a girl, it's a fact,
it's the love of my life.
She is nice on the eyes,
but she's never my wife.

2/13/2009

Water on the chalkboard
is a bomb in the city.
In death we are cleaned,
but it never is pretty.
So take this old soul,
Lord, over the waves,
and love me forever
so I know that I'm saved.
We're a mess on the page,
a smudge of black ink
and we only get bigger
when we overthink.

Le jour où j'ai embrassé la luxure au revoir
2/14/2009

You are a symbol,
a symbol of lust,
for there is no love
or intimate trust.
I was addicted,
in love with a thought;
a promise of nothing,
a freezing robot.

loosening lips like alcohol
Feb. 22nd, 2009 at 10:09 PM

"When you sit by the fire," says Dave, "you talk more. You think deeper. It's sorta like a natural alcohol that you can enjoy when you're under 21. In the summer, you have a fire, then lay in the street after midnight when no cars come, and look up at the stars, and you have good talks because you're facing the same way. You both look at the fire and face the same way. You both lay on your backs and look up at the stars and you're facing the same way."

We were both lying on our backs and looking up at the stars and facing the same way. We had just had a fire and had some good conversation. That's the way it goes in high school. You don't plan on a night working out so beautifully simple. You just show up at Dave's house for a fire in his metal fire pit and see what happens. All the people from school show up and you make s'mores. Then they leave and Dave makes smoothies. In February. A warm night in February, and no one is looking for smoothies and a fire, but that's what you get.

"The universe seems so small when you sit by a fire. This abstract movement of something you can't touch, you can just feel it and enjoy its dance." We talk about girls, marriage, and getting older. We're scared. No senior tells a sophomore that they're scared. It doesn't work like that. Seniors have it all figured out when they're at school. But take them to a fire and see them weep. The honesty of the burning wood evokes something wetter than youth on the cheeks of the hardened seniors. We've seen it all. We know where we're going next year even when we haven't picked a college, or even started looking.

We talk about dances.

We talk about music.

There's smoke in my skin and a new fire in my eyes. After the hours of hearing nothing but the pop and snap of the wood and the "Fireside

Music" playlist, it's hard to think about bed. People wouldn't be so tired if they sat by more fires. Watching the energetic flow of the flames fills you with something that words can't. It makes me want to dance. It makes me want to sing.

I have to leave. I was supposed to be home by twelve and it's twelve o nine. Dave and I are lying in the street talking about summer. In February. I have the mountains. I want a beach. Dave wants a beach in the mountains.

"That would be cold," I said.

"Not if it was at sea level."

"Then they wouldn't be mountains."

"Yes they would. Mountains in the ocean."

I have to drive home. The bad thing about high school is still having a curfew, because these are the kinda nights that you wouldn't mind chasing into in the morning. You wouldn't mind not falling asleep. These are the kinda nights that inspire books that inspire movies.

So I drive home singing a song I made up and can't stop smiling. I have a 'life smile' on because mine is very much happening and I seem to be right in the midst of it. No one warned me about nights like these that define high school.

We go to school for seven hours, work for five, then sit by a fire for one and remember the fire. That's how it is. An image burned into my cranium.

And I don't mind the heat.

- **Current Mood:** Poetic

2/22/2009
(Evidently written when I thought Colorado was a Midwestern state)

A day derived of poetry
and landlocked lakes presiding,
let sleep slip through cold fingers
in the dreary, dead midwest.

Dream of summer's sing song melody
to bric-a-brack gathering brains,
and love-lost open firewood
by flame's first fleeting dance.

And sing low, oh glory,
Jesus, my best friend
in prairie's lonely winter days,
Your faithfulness won't end.

The Thinkers, they think.
That is their job,
and that is all they do.
They never move
or have ideas.
Never do they speak,
and never do they sleep.
The Thinkers think,
and that is all.
They never eat
or drink.
Never do they make merry,
laugh, cry, or excrete.
The Thinkers, they think.
Thinking is their job,
and they are good at what they do.
The Thinkers, they think
and that is all.

2/25/2009

Without air,
caged birds die
just as quickly
as free birds.
We are a sky
drowning in clouds.
In a flurry of
sunlight, we draw
our last breath.
Dance now,
dance in the yellow
and pink rays.
Swirl as the wind blows
and wander alone
to the ground
as rain.

3/1/2009

To adhere to location
or dance in one place;
I have done both now
for most of my days.
Release,
release,
oh please,
release and let wander
my feet where they may.
Turn the wheels of the car
across the
miles
and
miles
of gray.

cold floor

A few nights before I went to Massachusetts, I was texting Natalie late at night. We got onto the topic of the future and what we want to do. I mentioned that I may want to go to Europe or Africa and teach missionary kids, like my cousin did. I talked about moving back to the Cape and going to college out there. We talked about the freedom of the road and just going and "leaving all your troubles behind, at least for a few hours," as she put it. It was way past my bedtime, but I was so entranced in the conversation and my mind was going and going about all the millions of things I could do with my life. I was reminded of the segment in The Curious Case of Benjamin Button, after he leaves his wife and baby and wanders around doing and being different things. I told her about how thoroughly I would enjoy that lifestyle. She agreed and talked about how she would love to be a missionary and travel the world and, ironically to me, how sick she is of the Cape. That night, I began to look at the future not as something to be terrified of, but to embrace and to be excited for. My mind was still running faster than any American highway would ever allow, and I wanted to go to Africa. And Europe. It felt like I was leaving tomorrow. Lost in conversation and the wanderings of my mind, I got up to go to the bathroom.

I put my feet on the cold floor

and reality sadly drudged back into my head.

I had school in the morning.

And the day after that.

- **Current Mood:** Fluorescent

3/17/2009 am

There's a tree on a hill
that reminds me of you.
Could be the way that you dressed,
like the sky wearing blue.
I'm so far from the ocean,
my shining blue sea.
If you were the east,
the west would be me.
It's so hard to exist
in this land-shackled state.
I always miss you,
but more so as of late.

3/22/2009

Oh musical note,
how you get stuck in my head
with the way that you dance,
a staticky thread.
Let go of my coast,
you crashing waves of blue!
Release my mind to wander
from a single thought of you.
A ravenous strand—
the hair from your mind.
Let's not wander too far
into this surprise gold mine.

I don't know your name
or recall where we met,
but I'm lost in your eyes
so I tend to forget
that there's nothing as deep,
no river so rich
as your bright, sunny smile
when the metaphor fits.
You've got a tune in your step
and a sea in your hair
and that makes it much worse
when I'm not out there.
Because your summer was ours
by the echoing blue
with the ponds and the sea
and me sitting by you.

Math
Undated song, Spring 2009

There's a place in my heart
where I love to hate school
and e'rybody I know says
I'll turn out a fool.
I don't listen to them,
they don't know me like you,
whom I call on the phone
when I am feeling blue.
Help me stand, help me up,
we can play in the snow.
There's this dream I keep having
where I have to let go.
I've been turning to you
way more often than not
but I have to hang up
'cause you're not what I thought.

> *(Chorus)*
> Doo-do-do-do
> They're teaching us math
> Doo-do-do-do
> They're calling on me
> Doo-do-do-do
> They're teaching us math
> Doo-do-do-do
> They say that I cheat

With a powerful essay,
I rewrote the skies
and got kicked out of school
but at least I did try.
The art of a language
is not that hard to master,
even I can do it
and I'm a disaster.
From your place on the dock
where we once held hands,
you looked at the stars
and said you understand
all the things you weren't taught
while sitting in class;
deeper things of this world
are not that hard to grasp.
In a letter you wrote
in two thousand and eight,
you said Colorado
is not your home state.

(Chorus)

At the Zoo
3/25/2009 am

I saw the giraffes and
the elephants from way far away
and sent a picture to you
of them.
I saw gorillas
and monkeys and
grizzlies and snakes.
I laughed and I looked,
I pointed and 'oohed,'
but most of the time
from my day at the zoo
were hours and hours
spent thinking of you.

4/1/2009

The past is gone
but I'm so small
I look backward
and see it all.
Forgiving like
the Son of Man
is so much easier
said than done.
But I will love
and leave the past
as it should be
in piles of ash.
Because I've my own
and you have yours;
by now I should
have shut the doors.

4/3/2009

Every night—
or morning, I should say—
at about ten past twelve,
I hear Dakota get
up from her bed,
walk to her bowl,
and drink loudly
until she is content.
Then she returns
to her peace,
as do I.

I've been up far later
than I should be
lately.
At work, I sing.
We are seeds
blowing toward each other
and when we meet,
we bloom.
And in our hybrid blossom,
are beautiful.

I like you.

4/6/09

Goodnight, my drifting
tumbleweed,
with cares afar
and spirit free.
For in my mind,
the fences crowd
with tumbling dry
weeds gathered 'round.
You've held my foot
in lovesick snare,
yet clung to joy
without a care.
Oh, tumbleweed,
we are the same
so dance with me
into the flame.

Perspective
4/8/2009

I like it
I like it
I like it a lot

It's only
the feeling
of something just bought.

4/14/2009 am

I'd miss you
if we'd never met,
but since we have
I can't forget
the way you talk
and write to me,
where every line
is poetry.
The softest laugh,
the gentle smile
through telephones
across the miles
only makes me
miss you more,
it's so much greater
than before.

4/26/2009

Reaching this year's turning point,
I have to turn my back.
Do Mommy's hands smell the nicest
or am I just feeling trapped?
Should I just try to ignore
the feelings I've been looking for,
or is this really it? Are you just my…

I'm thinking about times we talked
while the snow is coming down.
You're at a party on Cape Cod
with your good friends gathered 'round.
The point is that I miss you,
though we never talked that much.
I'd just like to be near you
in a never ending touch.

5/26/2009

Am I a poet
or am I just dressed like one?
Am I an artist
or am I drawing for fun?

If I were the sky
with the clouds as my paint,
I would paint you a scene
which would make your heart race.

As my sun slowly set
o'er the liveliest sea,
I would merely be glad
you were looking at me.

i grew up.
Jun. 30th, 2009 at 4:48 PM

I don't think I've ever had a moment like this before.

I was talking to Anna, laying in the field, and I suddenly grew up. I felt older than I had before. She told me she's pregnant and I had to let go of her forever in that way. I told Matt I'd take good care of them, and he seems like a good kid, but it will never be the same between Anna and I. I think it will be better. More mature. Less petty.

So we'll see how everything works out.

7/4/2009 am

These hundred thousand
acre woods
are all so lost
and all so good.

We held our hands
inside these woods
and kissed our lips;
I wasn't good.

I held you close
inside these woods,
these hundred thousand
acre woods.

But now you're lost,
just as you would,
you lost me here
within these woods.

The Fisherman
7/4/2009

I'm confused
on what to do
about this kiss
and about you.

You see these men,
these gorgeous men,
you fish with them
so late and then,

'neath fireworks
and little perks
when I'm not there
and you're "at work,"

I do not know,
or want to know
the things you do
or where you go.

7/16/2009

I don't get
why I always fail myself,
and I am not alone
in who I disappoint.

And despite all bad things
said of me,
you like or love me
nonetheless.

7/17/2009

In the airport, with these eternal jets,
they leave and come and so do i,
as if one of them.
i am airplanes.
i am they,
i fly through air
and go away

(Unfinished?)

7/18/2009

Beneath the sky next to the sea,
I held your hand and held my breath
as comets passed and dark waves danced,
I wondered what's inside your head.
(You said) don't you always feel so small
to look upon celestial beings?
(I said) not really, it's not so bad
I know the Guy who made those things.

7/25/2009

There's a spider in the window
and a fly up on the wall
and I hear you talking to me
and I hear nothing at all.
And there's some blood on both of my hands
and a cut on both my knees
and I think I'd see you sooner
if you weren't so hard to please.
And there's a song that's stuck in my head
and a picture in my mind
and I do not know what I would do
if I left our love behind.

dakota

Aug. 11th, 2009 at 12:15 PM

I don't know what time she died, but it happened today. When I first heard that they had to put her down, I cried for the first time in years. I can't even remember the last time I cried before that. Presently, I can't think of a proper way to commemorate her life and how much she meant to me and how much I'll miss her. She is the only one I've ever known who never said a single harmful thing to or about me or anyone. I guess that's why they're man's best friend.

I'm gonna miss ya, pooch. I always loved you, and be a good girl. Maybe we'll bump into each other in heaven some day.

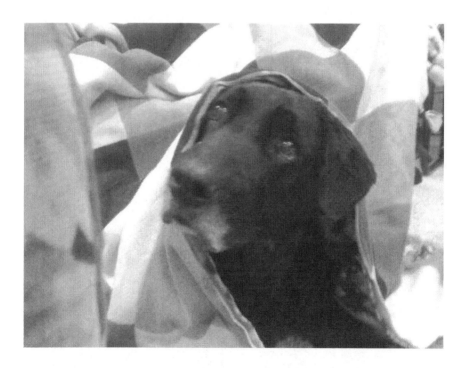

The Day You Died
8/11/2009

It rained, it rained
out of the sky
oh, how it poured
the day you died.
I wept, the tears
fell from my eyes,
oh, how I mourn
the day you died.
The angels fell,
and let out cries,
oh, how they hurt
the day you died.
And I was lost,
I broke inside,
oh, how I loathe
the day you died.

For Zac
8/31/2009

We row 'neath the sun
in our half-sunk canoes
and you point out the sky
as it comes into view.

and then one day,
the rain came

Sep. 14th, 2009 at 12:44 AM

Then one day, the rain came. It stayed with us for a few days until someone else deserved it more than we did. No one walked anywhere or rode their bikes. Cars drove slowly and honked their horns more.

The third day of the rain, I walked to the library and found that they had closed 15 minutes prior to my arrival. I walked home from the library in the pouring rain. I enjoyed the sound of my shoes hitting the ground like wet towels beside a pool. My glasses were in need of windshield wipers, and my shirt was heavy.

I continued walking, not seeing the circumstance as a bad thing, but as an opportunity to enjoy a moment with God, in His beautiful creation. In fact, I was a little reluctant to enter my house and end the little moment with the Creator. I went in, hung up my sopping clothes, and got ready for work.

Passengers
9/15/2009

and then at night, i own these streets,
at night these streets are mine.
at night there are no passengers
to say i cannot drive.
within the wraps of darkness came
a freedom so sincere,
within the wraps of darkness came
a word i couldn't hear.
so when at night, you're on these streets,
out driving past your time,
abandon ship, you Wagon Wheel,
you know these streets are mine.

9/21/2009

Curveball number three:
I need you like the sun.
I know that we only met a few days ago
for real,
but I don't know what to think.
I fall in love
every other day,
but what is this?

a run-on night
Sep. 23rd, 2009 at 11:31 PM

Because we felt a little hungry atop the Bay School in Osterville, I suggested that we drive to Denny's, because it was so late that that would be the only place to get food after our jam session (followed by playing in the gym) going up to both attics, and then breaking and entering, so they agreed and after suggesting we take Natalie's car (which I still feel awful about), we headed off in the black Camry, hit a gas station once we were over the bridge, where the owner looked at me suspiciously for running around the building looking for a hose with which to wash off my feet, and rolled on to the place we would not see that day, called Denny's, and the cause for this absence of food was whatever Natalie ran over on I-195, a mile and a half outside of Westport, because her tire went flat, she called AAA, and we waited around for them to come, and by the time they did, we had decided to phone for a police officer to come and give us a ride to the nearest town, so we did and he arrived there shortly, providing all three of us our first ride in a police car, the 4 miles to the only gas station that was open, where we met Eric, who was funny and a little creepy at the same time, and wished us well as we headed out the door to walk to no where in particular, but we ended up stumbling across this "adult apartment complex," walking around it, and discovering a lake with a city on the other side that we absolutely had to walk to, so we set off in that direction, but stopped at a gazebo outside of a Holiday Inn, where Courtney and I left Natalie to continue our quest to the unnamed city, which actually turned out to be Fall River, which has one of the coolest office buildings ever, called 'Meditech,' with bright colors and cool windows, and about two miles beyond it, we found some town houses and decided to turn around because Natalie had texted me and said that she walked to her car and was staying in it, which at this point sounded lovely to us, because we had walked about 5 miles by now and wanted nothing more than to sit down, so we turned around and opted this time to walk on some overgrown train tracks by the side of the lake, which ended up running into a dead end, so we were forced to once more turn around and get back to the sidewalk on the side of the highway, and that is when my heart stopped because I saw the most realistic 'shadow person' ever, and swore he was real until I got closer and realized it was just a bush, so we pressed on, got back to the gas station, stopped to get some donuts and milk, because their morning delivery had come by since our last visit, and proceeded to walk the 3 mile trek to where Natalie's car was, but which we forgot the name of, so we stopped at a few other car-ish looking places to see if her car was in any of their lots, which it wasn't, which only led us to more walking, and by the time we did get to the tire shop where she and her car were, the sun was starting to rise over a cloud blanketed sky, and we were so relieved to sit down, but we could not fall asleep because we had to wait 26 more minutes, so it was a whole 24 hours that we were awake for, since Courtney and I had woken up at 6 the day before to go work out, and we made it groggily, then passed out, and apparently Natalie couldn't fall asleep because of my snoring, so instead, she just took a video of me snoring and put it on Facebook for the world to regard with awe, and two hours later, we had to evacuate the car to allow the kind mechanics to swap the tires, and just like that, we were off to home, which, despite the hour-long drive, went by pretty quickly in my opinion, and I was dropped off first at 9:30am, which is when I realized that I had spent the entire last 12 hours with Natalie and Courtney, having a blast.

9/24/2009 ac

This is as much fun
as we will ever have,
and I would predict our future
if I could only see the past.
We don't run through all the sprinklers
and expect to just stay dry,
just like you don't walk along this ground
without falling from the sky.
If there is only one for me
(and I truly hope there is)
then I don't see, with all my might,
how she could be better than this.
We're the forest in the mountains,
and the rain that washed the sand.
We're the train along the train tracks;
boy and girl gone hand in hand.
And I sing your name cross country,
as I run from coast to coast,
with every letter ringing
just as loudly as the last.
If we have found a path to joy,
a road beyond reproach,
then let me take you to the place
that I admire most.
We'll take a boat
across the bay
and waste a
perfectly fine day
just singing, talking, digging deep
I won't remember
what secrets to keep.
But there's a flaw in my plan,
there's this one other man,
and beyond what I feel,
I just must understand

that you were his first,
oh, disheartening pines,
where the flag bearers fell
from their pre-posted lines.
I'll hold onto your hand,
I will stand by your side
until this cheap little boy
is saluting goodbye.
But these are my dreams,
and I know I'll move on
through the valleys of longing
where the poets have gone
to search for a lover,
perhaps yet a second
to pamper their whims
and to come when they're beckoned.

9/30/2009

Breathe in smoky air,
breathe it out.
Vanilla.
Honey.
The thickened air by my lips,
cracking,
tasty,
smoky.
The roof of the school
by the parking lot light,
the cigars hung from lips
as the police drove right by.
Coughing and cracking,
burning paper on our fingertips.
He's a pro. Such a smoker.
And I will do this again
when I forget how much it hurts.
Fear inside a closet,
a lifeless body.
We can live like this.

10/17/2009

nothing says i love you
like saying i love you.

i love you.

10/23/2009

Let's travel, let's go,
we will see sand and snow,
we'll wander the deserts
and be a good show.

They'll film us for TV,
they'll sell off our stamps,
they'll look up and see us
parading like champs.

There will be no ending,
we'll walk to our tombs,
and live on forever
in God's biggest rooms.

Dogtown
11/15/2009
Previously published in Poetry for the Mind's Joy, *The Poetry
and Literature Center at the Library of Congress*

let me scribble with the pen:
i am no legend,
let me not breathe,
i am not great.
drink it on the store tops;
these boys are heroic.
they tear the swimmers
from the pools and
spill themselves in, water.
bleed until the ink sinks in,
these words are freedom,
these frames are legacy.
hold us down with your words;
blind us with your fluorescent bulbs,
your eyes are not the sun
and your mouth is not a chain
so scream it loud
and stare all you want.
it's freedom and it's loud.

My Girl In Ashes
11/19/2009

My girl would be thirteen today,
my girl would be so old.
I'd see her running in the yard
if she weren't turning cold.
Her ashes lying on my desk.
Her ashes in my hand.
My girl is gray and powdered soot,
I hope she understands
that as she sits upon my desk,
upon her final throne,
I'll throw her to the wind but still
she'll never be alone.

on the faded rose

Dec. 2nd, 2009 at 1:24 AM ad

I knew that this would happen,
that you'd leave me all alone,
but I can't blame you for looking,
hoping that I'd make it home.
But there is no silver lining,
and there is no snowing day
when families are all at the tree
just a-smiling away.
So I did decide to do something
about how I am alone.
I'll drive far from this coastal line
and I won't pick up the phone.
I will not think of her today,
or tomorrow or the next,
about how how she swept me off my feet,
and then she broke my neck…
Or was it slightly lower,
was it a burning in my chest?
The flames that burn whole cities down
and cause me such unrest.
They spread into my blood and veins;
I feel them in my eyes,
they burn up my appendages
and tear me up inside.
I'll fondly miss your pounding waves
off beaten, battered shores,
pressed up against the sandy night,
I'll fade into the roar.

felony

Dec. 9th, 2009 at 8:44 AM

I write this in the hopes that the wrong eyes do not fall upon it. Last night, I was with Amanda (ahhhh...melting like butter) and we decided to enter the old, condemned Osterville Elementary School building, as I have many times before. At one point, she put her hand on my back!! We went up on the roof and she was loving it, the adventurous soul.

Then a cop pulled up.

"Shoot!"

We rushed down as fast as we could and called out to him, although we could have gotten away (but he had my plates down already; next time, park at the library, or in a group of cars). He had us sit in the parking lot for half an hour.

Another cop pulls up. More sitting.

Fifteen minutes later, another cop pulls up. They look around the school, occasionally wandering over to get information from us. However, during the lengthy lapses in which we are not being interrogated, we're making jokes and laughing. As she put it, "at least we got some good bonding time in."

Eventually, we were let off the hook because we made ourselves known, but he said there is a chance that we could get something in the mail. Bottom line: "Trespassing is a felony. If you don't own it, you don't go on it."

PS, I now know the reason the mannequin was in the closet: Police training.

- **Current Music:** The Maine, 'Whoever She Is'

12/20/2009

This is fighting
in the literal sense,
this is where you sent
your dollars and cents.
This is where the
yellow sun bleeds,
and this is where all
men are machines.
All battered and bloody,
they come like it's Sunday
to throw around blows
and gather up money.
This is the life
that I never have lived,
yet I act everyday
like the toughest of kids.

12/22/2009

Terminal,
you're taking me away.
Lines on boxes
taxi while I wait,
and if I could take it back,
if I could do it all again,
you'd be wearing those leaves
like a rhododendron.

You're the summer sky,
you are the darkest white,
you painted with the clouds
then you rained goodbye.
You are the freest bird,
you are the love of earth,
and when I'm feeling low,
you are the kindest word.

There's a silence in the air
when I'm that high off the ground,
the kind we liked to talk about
when we used to hang around.
And there's a robot in the skies
who is smiling in the blue,
it is taking me wherever—
near to anyone but you.

Taylour
Dec. 22nd, 2009 at 3:19 PM

Oh, daughter of the heavens,
have you not those angel wings?
Cannot you fly to Africa
or Europe with those things?

But why do you lie fallen,
down there sleeping in the dirt,
crying like you're broken,
like a segment of a worm?

Take off like Dakota,
or the grapes beneath the press.
However you go down,
I think you do it best.

You're the purest in the form,
but you're missing what's inside.
You're the beauty of a furnace
when the fires have all died.

today; Christmas Eve

Dec. 25th, 2009 at 1:25 AM

Luke and I went sledding/snowboarding on the crest of the Rockies. Perfect powder dressed the golden hills as he led me to this spot he had found that no one else knew about. And he was right. The snow was as virgin as me. The hill he led me to, however, was huge and steep. So I stomped into my board and took off at the starting pace of mach one. After accelerating for a few seconds, I caused myself to fall—not because I lost my balance or hit anything, but because I was going fast and instinctively ceased the motion.

An hour later, as we trekked back to the car half a mile away, I wondered why we are wired to fear motion. I basically had two football fields to go before reaching the rocks at the bottom, so why make myself stop moving so quickly? It is not out of fear of physical harm, but more out of a fear of motion, or too much happening at once.

And, as was inevitably seen coming, this applies to my life. I have no clue what awaits me at the bottom, and I am in no hurry to get there. I simply want to enjoy the ride down. And I make myself stop. I am not stuck anywhere by anyone's decisions but my own.

Note to self: Let go and move on,

there are bigger reef to hide in in the oceans of the world.

Go.

Christmas
12/25/2009

Take the birth of Jesus
and turn it oh so gentle,
turn it into all the things
He turned over in the temple.

2010

THE DREAMER INTERNATIONAL

I flew from Colorado back to Cape Cod after Christmas break.

I was still living with Arlette, the French lady, and would for the rest of my time on Cape Cod. It continued to be a lonely season, as I lived alone and did not have a plethora of close friends.

As winter gave way to spring however, I gathered a small crew of people who would go on some crazy adventures with me before I headed down to Australia. Cinco de Mayo, described in full detail below, was one of the wildest days of my life, and I have only fond memories of TD, Amanda and Natalie.

Early in the year, I had decided to pursue a school with Youth With A Mission (YWAM), which started in Australia, then went to a handful of other countries. So after a quick couple weeks back in Colorado in June, I was on my way to the southern hemisphere. I would spend three months on the Sunshine Coast of Australia, then one in Thailand and one in India. We then went back to Australia and split up. I stopped in New Zealand on my way back to the States and got to visit Hobbiton (Mata-Mata), but sacrificed Thanksgiving with my family to sightsee by myself.

It was a sharp learning curve to fit into community and put others before myself. Because I was a little 19-year-old twerp, I didn't make many friends on this trip, but that doesn't mean it was bad. Far from it. It matured me and humbled me and set not only an adventurous course for the rest of my life, but a spiritual one as well...

so we cause some trouble,
throw some stones,
break some windows,
break some bones.
in whose name do we pray?
and whose fault is all this?
well, he brings division,
he warned us all of this.

so we drive a tad fast
and we talk to some girls,
and we do not wear watches,
we've all the time in the world,
but whose kingdom should come
and whose name do we bear?
why, it's Christ, the Anointed,
who else can compare?

Gaining Weight
1/16/2010

Balance the heart while we drive on this coast
and I'll show you a cancer they can't diagnose.
Now some call it love, and some others, disease,
and you know I'd be yours if you'd only said please.
You're an ocean of soul; you're a heart wrapped in gold;
you're a desert on fire that will never grow cold.
So tell me your secret and sell me a tale
and I'll weave you a basket for your bread and some ale
and forever, we'll run, oh, we'll run through the streams,
we'll splash through the rivers where fishermen dream.
We'll dash over prairies and hills made of bronze
where the locals play ball with the deer and their fawns.
Oh together, we'll soar. We will fly through the clouds.
We'll hike about valleys and wander around.
So tell me you're with me and we can go now,
but don't tell me to wait 'cause I just don't know how.

1/19/2010
A Rap

i'ma travel i'ma soar,
i'ma hit 'em with this roar,
they can see me
on the TV,
they can come and ask for more,
i'm the next dead president,
an envelope's resident,
the borderlines, the boys with spines,
they tell me where the press is at,
run the beach, identity,
'cause grace could save a wretch like me,
there is no truer entity
than Jesus Christ my G-O-D.

so i'ma travel, i'ma go,
i'm hit them with this flow,
you arrest me,
and you stress me,
just a cough so don't ca-bless me,
if you find you're lacking fun,
just ask the Wayne man, he has tons,
they call him symbol, call him god,
he's just an idol, he will fall,
as if he's representing Judah,
like a lion in the flock.
misleading kids to smoke the bark,
to burn it up like Joan of Arc,
and if you're fighting, tell a kid,
'cause they call him the little narc.

the eventful run

Jan. 20th, 2010 at 3:38 PM

I stood on the edge of the shallows, arms raised to the heavens. I sang thanks to the One who made me and started heading home. I had run the sand at Craigville after the mile-long run to get there. I had seen the rain turn to snow for a few minutes before it changed its mind and returned to rain. There is no amount of adjectives I could throw at the beauty of the Cape in the winter. Or the summer or fall, for that matter.

After passing the water on my way home, I see a car up the road come to a halt in the middle of the street. I glanced ten feet to the right and there was a fox running on the side of the road. The car moved on, but I broke into a sprint toward the animal. He watched me approach through bandit's eyes. I slowed to a walk and knelt down. I spoke alien tongues comprised of whistles and clicks, but he didn't understand me and edged back toward the woods, home. Still confused, he turned from me and began to trot away. He glanced back once more, his eyes questioning what I had to offer him. I continued to watch until he slipped behind a knoll and was gone. Inspired by the fox's curiosity, I sprinted home, demolishing my figurative 'runner's wall.'

- **Current Mood:** apathetic
- **Current Music:** Augustana: 'All the Stars and Boulevards'

79

I'm writing you a letter.
so you'd better be excited.
I'm hoping that it's better
than the last one that I writed.
I'm writing you a letter
and I'm sending you some songs,
that I could sing forever
of my Savior and my God.
I'm writing you a letter
and I'll use some metaphors.
They'll put you in a shredder
and you'll see what men are for.
I'm writing you a letter
oh, it's gonna be so grand.
I'll tell you that you're better
than the best I've ever had.

love, ethan.

a little freaked out

I don't know if anyone else does this, but I've begun to look at married couples—particularly those around my parents' age—and look at how they interact. Tonight, game night at the Kendall's house, I began hoping that my wife and I will be as funny together as my and Kendall's parents are. I want to show up to a party/gathering of any sort with her and be the couple that people love to invite; the people who bounce off each other so well that there is no doubt they were knit for each other.

I have a person in mind who would fit this criteria, and I can only pray that she thinks similarly of me. The more I think and pray and reflect about her, the more I realize that I need her, or her DNA carbon copy, in my life. Maybe that is slightly extensive, but I know what I'm looking for in "the one" and she has it. She has it down cold.

Is it strange that I think about my spouse so much? Do any of you? I think it's important to start thinking now about the person I'm dying to spend the rest of my life with, and maybe I am slightly aggressive in doing so, but I think it's a good thing. For now, I'll keep on praying for her, and for me— that I'll be the husband she deserves.

On a side note, I ran about five miles today on the C-470 trail at the mile high elevation and just about died. But now I feel super good. And my future self is going to hate me for staying up so late, since I have to get up at 6 tomorrow for worship practice.

Life.

Gotta love it.

- **Current Music:** Alison Krauss

2/20/2010

Wake up.
Sleep.
Et cetera.

2/23/2010

Up before tomorrow
like the day we beat the dawn,
I found for you a sunrise
and I put it in this song.

I'll run through woods on barefoot
with some friends who love me, yet,
I'd rather run with you
so I can get my sneakers wet.

You are all the Rocky Mountains.
You're those glowing purple peaks,
you're the burning in my calves
and you're the song that makes me weak.

2/24/2010

i know
  of a river
   running like
    the toys that
    just wind up
    and go. you
     hold me next
    to this body
    and sing in
   to my ear
  oh, come
  on lauren
 are you
waiting
for me?
i   know
i   have
sa   id this
bef   ore, but
now,   now i'm
begi   nning to
long.   sister, will
you   let me l
on   g for
y   o
u   ?

googly

Mar. 2nd, 2010 at 7:12 PM aa

Inside and out
when we're singing amazing grace at the top of our lungs in the showers,
when we're speeding on our way to wicked; you're checking out Arthur and
we're blowing each other's brains.
When we're worshipping God on our hands and knees,
when we glorify Him with our tongues.
When we're watching surf videos till 2am on your family's couch
when we're sipping Starbucks tied to chairs and we try to beat you at the
memory game.
I love it when we're Scrub Scrabbling and your words stab my eyes
(oh how they love to breathe)
and when we're running after midnight through a silent traffic light.
When I come down to visit, I hope you'll let me stay a while.
I hope you plan on staying for a very long while.
Or when I scare you like a girl and make you spill your coffee.
When my teacher calls me a homophobe (I'm not) and I'm shining in her
visage.
Or right now,
when I'm driving to your house and my shuffle knows me all too well,
I'll drunken dial—drunk with love—and hang up after a second.
But you know me all too well,
maybe better than my iPod,
and then I sing loudly and go up the stairs.

•   **Current Music:** Flatfoot 56

3/10/2010

Somewhere between us
is a road to the shore,
somewhere between us
is a road to nowhere.

I see your eyes, yes
your windows to the world.
I see your eyes and
wish you could be my girl.

Because somewhere between us
is a road yet to drive;
a stone's throw from the waters
we have yet to dive.

3/11/2010

Still I speak
in the words of the singer;
my words on his tongue,
they passed through my mind
but a second too late.
So now you call me
a copycat,
and rightly so, my dear friend.
After all, are we all not
memorizations of a lifestyle,
cascading through our actions
toward an ocean in the ground?

PenPal!

So I have a confession to make. I received your postcard today. I said that I would start this letter several days ago, but never did, as I have not been home before 10 or 11 at night lately and I've been SO busy and didn't get around to it. SO SORRY! But here it is.

Lately, my life has become quieter. The music I listen to while driving dictates what kind of mood I'm in. I doubt anyone who rides with me would notice, but if they observed which songs I played and which ones I skipped on my iPod Shuffle, they could tell a lot about my mood. For the past week or so, Iron & Wine's "The Trapeze Swinger" has been the theme song of my life, so here's what I'm doing: I'm playing it on repeat the entire time I'm writing this letter so that maybe, just maybe, it will seep through my syntax.

I was incredibly encouraged the other day by a guy who models at Abercrombie with me. We started talking one night while closing up the store. The next day, he added me on Facebook and popped up a chat window saying, "You're a Christian?? Now way! That is SOO COOL!" I thanked him and asked why. He said that he is too and I got pumped up. He posts Bible verses a lot and I am just so excited that I'm not alone there. It's very awesome.

Tonight, I just returned from a do-se-do. It was easily the most fun I've had at church in a long time. There was a contest for the best cornbread, pie, and chili, and I entered a cornbread with cinnamon crust an honey bread. It was delicious and all my friends thought I'd win but I didn't. It was my first time taking food to a potluck!

(I have to be honest, I just changed the music to some Crooked Still and Sarah Harmer—Great folk music!)

Then we played Family Feud and danced. All the old-time music made me long for a Southern summer night, dancing under flickering lanterns to hand claps, foot stomps, and one mean violin or fiddle. Summer tends to thrust me into a folk music binge, and I guess this is a great kick-off for it!

I long to be eaten by bugs while rolling down a deep green hill, or picking dirt off a juicy slice of watermelon accidentally dropped on the ground. I heard Garrison Keillor whispering one of his epic tales from

Lake Wobegone and swear I smelt the apple rhubarb pie sitting fresh on the stove. There's something so beautifully simple about the humidity drowning the muted steps of an Alabama square dance. I could say that part of my desire to roam the world (ironically) is to find this simplicity. Like Tom Cruise's character in the end of *The Last Samurai*, I want to seek peace on this earth.

(Unfinished)

careful

Mar. 13th, 2010 at 12:20 AM

I love A Prairie Home Companion
and Garrison Keillor
and hope
and sun eyed girls
and Louise Deutsch DeSantis
and Florida
and housesitting
and TD because he gets me
and couscous french toast
and running till I can't breathe
and hope
hope
but more than these
God
and also, you know who
if you know who you are

•   **Current Music:** A Prairie Home Companion

A Dream from Spring, 2010
(Recorded 11/7/2012)

This is likely the most memorable and formative dream I have ever had. I awoke that morning shaken, not necessarily because of the abundance of events in the dream, for the plot is rather simple, but because of the depth, richness, and general mood of the dream. The atmosphere and emotion were pure and vibrant, as was the immediate sense of intimacy I felt with the woman, and I still get shivers when I look back on it.

I sailed up to the shore of this exotic new continent and saw her silhouetted on the dock against a vibrant gold dusk sky. Behind her a couple yards stood her sister, who would silently observe as we spoke. I knotted the 8 around the cleat and rose to meet her.

She wore a light silver silk robe which hung loosely over her frame. A breeze flapped the fabric about her breast and her black hair across her face. She was not 'gorgeous' in the vein of supermodels or exotic famous actresses, but rather exuded a sort of muted beauty which radiated through her simplicity.

"I'm Ethan," I said as I took her velvet hand.

She told me her name, which by now I've forgotten.

I asked if she would like to join me as I sail around the world and she nodded. Stooping to pick up the packed suitcase at her ankle, she looked back at her sister once more in a silent farewell glance.

A lightning bolt of eager joy shot down my spine as I led her to the ship. We stepped over the lip of the hull and onto the wooden bridge. We pushed off from the dock and as we sail into the coming night, she never looks back at the life she is leaving behind. Instead, she looks forward into the world yet to be discovered. She is satisfied to follow her captain and eager to remain by his side.

Yet the sun never sets and the golden sky lingers.
Night never arrives in the glory of this dream world.
My girl and I embark across the
ocean beneath a permanent sunset sky.

4/1/2010 akb

I'm searching for the full moon,
but I'm finding only teeth
knocked out of a smiling mouth
sunk down onto the reef.

They clattered, tingling, in the surf,
they scattered o'er the tide
and though attempts were made to rescue,
the molars sailed till sunrise.

I wept upon such loss as this,
such beauty thrown to sea,
but anchors cast and sails at rest,
I finally set you free.

4/3/2010

Watching light wrap 'round your body,
the beautiful figure that God gave you,
I lose the purity of the moment
and put more nails into my Savior.

Singing songs out loud while driving,
I'm feeling lost behind the wheel,
I stop and wait at every green light
wondering if you're really real.

So questions, answers come and go
and I'm left amidst the dust
that settles slowly 'round your fingers
dipping slowly into lust.

foot sweat

The average person's feet excrete several quarts of sweat a day. That is a strange way to say that life is beautiful down to every microscopic aspect of it. It's running back from a quick run to Cumberland Farms to my friends—some of the greatest people alive—playing football at 10 pm, surrounded by cars with their headlights shining on our tiny field. We're dirty. We're stinky. We want to sleep, but our brains are far beyond tired. Friday Football was finally a success today for the first time, but unfortunately, my experience at softball was not. But I still had a blast jumping up onto the bleachers and playing Pickle which I haven't played in years. It's days like these that you can't plan. Event coordinators are helpless to the extent of creating days as beautifully random as this one. Concluding at a bar at 1:30am with Amanda, I got caught thinking that sure, no one is perfect. Found out a few things about her that I didn't know before. But does that mean that they should be avoided at all costs? Quite the opposite. While snuggling with Tiddleywinks and Amanda staring up at the holes to heaven under her mongo blanket, we forced each other's brains to work much harder and much deeper than they had in a long time. We explored philosophy and sensual perception. What is it? No idea. But we talked about it. We marveled at the amazing double shooting stars we saw before the clouds conquered the sky. I laughed hard when we found out that Jeff realized the girl he's had a crush on is mentally handicapped. Love my life. With a rousing run this morning around the beautiful land surrounding the Kennedy Compound, followed by a blink of work, then football, then dinner with the people after some great car trips, followed by a softball game, and then ultimate frisbee and night football, this day is a success. I should not have to work weeks to receive a day like this. I should quit school. Quit my jobs. And live like this.

Oh wait,
I am.

- **Current Music:** The Middle East, 'Blood'

5/4/2010

And I ran until the ocean
had a battle with the shrouds
that blew away the rainfall,
taking rainbow with the clouds.

The diamonds fell through light
wherever sun had hit the drops;
illuminating rain
until it takes a breath and stops.

I ran by turgid ponds,
where the American plague is bred.
I stood atop a cold stone wall
over Cape Cod's buried dead.

They stared up through the soil,
begging me to see the sky,
but I was just a passerby
'neath God's blessing in disguise.

cinco de mayo
May 5th, 2010 at 9:23 PM (Written in 2012)

This
is one of those stories about one of those days that is permanently crystalized in your brain as one when whimsy and magic were not so far from reach. It is one of those days that, as the gray fog of time erodes away at the facts, it leaves a glossy imprint of a day that truly is too good to be true. Cinco de Mayo, 2010. I had never paid much thought to the importance of the Mexican holiday, and if I'm honest, still don't, but that date has a different sort of importance to me now. The type of weight that Disney tried to capture on the screen, and the freedom Twain stuffed into black words on a white page are the sorts of wonder that came alive to us on that day. A day that pressed pause on the pain and stresses of reality and opened the door to a world much kinder. There was no point to it, really.

Yah,
that was the day Amanda and I woke up early to go skating. I see that day in sepia, as the faded edges of my memory crystalize the day into a state of ancient film. We quickly grew hot and weary and set out to find the nearest beach. We ended up somewhere else, but didn't mind. We drove through this neighborhood of the wealthy upper class with stop signs at every cross streets and signs reminding me not to drive over their children who may be out playing in the streets. After tedious miles of neighborhood, the expanse of my blue Atlantic stretched herself out in front of us, arching her rigid back across the bed of sand. I scouted out a deserted stretch of beach from which to dive in and went for it. The hesitant Amanda stood on the beach and I called for her to come in. "I don't have a change of clothes!" she protested. I shouted some more, and she conceded. In her clothes and everything. That's when the term "anti-skinny dipping" tore into the world (*v: to enter the water fully clothed, and remove the wet articles upon emergence from the body of water*). We had no towels. We had no cares. The partly-nude Amanda and I climbed back into my car, soaking wet and happy.

Hang on,

Amanda was the surfer girl from the dreams I had when I envisioned exotic women in far off places. She grew up between Florida and Cape Cod, so her two passions were the sea, and being in it. I was dumbfounded by her blonde hair, oft pulled up by a flower near her ear; oh the way the sun kissed her head! I spent many sunsets seated next to her, strumming our wooden guitars and binding our hearts. Her toned frame hummed songs of freedom and the ocean, and I tended to simply sit idly by and watch. Her gentle voice was not from this century. It broke as she spoke of her parents and their separation; a fear she wrapped her own arms around regarding her future marriage.

But,

that was the day I dropped Amanda off at home and went to work in the office. It was the day I stared at the window the entire hour, longing to be on the other side of the pane. It was the day I left work hastily to grab Tyler and Natalie *(Tyler and Natalie; pl. n: the two best friends of mine while I lived on Cape Cod my first year of college. Fun-loving. Love to laugh. Can often be found hanging around our church youth group or mentoring high schoolers)*. We went to the supermarket and got yogurt. Tyler told us to leave him at the drug store so he could get a drink while we planted the yogurt in my fridge back home. Upon our return, we found him seated outside the automatic doors, dragging lazily on a cigarette. I popped my trunk and threw him inside (I did not want my car to smell like smoke!). We set off, Natalie and I in the front giggling, and TD in the trunk. As we screamed down Route 28, the light burned crimson on the lamp and we slowed, only to glance in the rearview mirror and see the Pollard girls in the car behind us. Not all of the Pollards, but all four girls, as the oldest had just obtained her license. I rang TD on his cellular. I told him I was about to pop the trunk and instructed him to sit up, smile and wave, and close the trunk again. I popped. I couldn't see what Tyler did, but I certainly saw the expressions on the Pollards' faces. Priceless. They're such sweet girls.

And,

that was the day we continued down 28 and saw a car accident, fresh out the oven. So fresh, in fact, the survivors were just now exiting their vehicles. The passing traffic slowed, but my Volkswagen pulled over to the side where a large woman stood with her arm around a small black girl; tears staining her Swiss chocolate cheeks. I asked if there was anything I could do and they said no. Both were still visibly shaking, and all I could do was offer them tissues from my car. It was then I remembered Tyler was still packed into my trunk. I released him from the trunk, to the surprise of all the slowly passing drivers, and he stood in the road. An officer from the police force drove up not half a minute after I let him out and started asking questions. We were just witnesses. We were okay. We left.

Food

was what we crafted the day the three of us drove away from the accident after being valiantly dismissed by the officer, and sped to Tyler's house. Once there, we hatched a plan to make the greatest dinner of all time. We caramelized onions, sliced fresh breads, meats and cheeses, diced crisp lettuce and tomatoes and arranged our sauces on Tyler's kitchen counter. We feasted on our creations. With stuffed mouths, we began planning for the night. Amanda got off work in an hour and a half. We agreed to kill time by heading South to the bay by Tyler's house, where we skipped from dock to dock, abrasively scooping moon jellyfish into buckets by the heaps. There were just so many of the suckers in the water that evening. The sun was lullabying itself to sleep behind the trees as we laughed on the wooden planks. We screamed, shouted, and photographed this evening. My best friends and I. We were lost. Carefree.

Oh,

that was the evening Natalie, Tyler, and I drove to Amanda's house. We crept up to her rear kitchen window, where she was making herself a bowl of ice cream at the counter. She looked at us and her heart leapt. She composed herself, paced to the door and let us in, wild and fearless. We told her to get ready, we were leaving. Amanda ran upstairs to make herself up, leaving the three of us awkwardly in her dining room with her parents. She returned. We were off. We had no idea where to, but that mattered to us as much as cabbage. Amanda guided us off the Cape via a route I'd never taken before. We drove around aimlessly and ended up exiting in Wareham, a town unfamiliar to all of us. Every May 5th was my childhood friend Kinsey's birthday, so after we called her and sang, we stumbled across a drained cranberry bog. In the pitch blackness, we could not determine its identity, and thought it was a pond. Therefore, we had to explore it. It was not a pond. Not two minutes after we pulled over to have a look though, an officer of the Wareham police force pulled up with his spotlight on us wading into the bog. We froze and returned to my vehicle. He commanded our identification of us, and told us to get on our way. We left, still not knowing where we were headed. But we knew one thing. The night was adolescent.

Of course,
that was the night we went to a gross bar called Shooters to inquire as to whether or not they serve food (didn't). Tyler ran in to ask and I moved the car. We laughed. We were intoxicated with the spirits of independent juvenescence. I gunned the car further astray and we soon found a Taco Bell. I parked a few spaces over from a car full of party people intoxicated with something *else*. Tyler, the socialite he is, struck up rapid conversation and found out that they were celebrating the fifth day of May with drugs, booze, and Taco Bell. The driver asked to talk to the two young women seated in my car, but Natalie and Amanda stayed put (Except to move into the driver's seat and try to move my car through the drive thru. Not knowing how to drive a standard, Amanda ran it up on the curb. Embarrassedly, they returned to their original seats and giggled). The kind folks donated two burritos to our night, wished us well, and drove away. Then Tyler and I looked up. We saw what we needed. What was required for our night.

Smoke.
That was the night we realized that the burritos we ate were probably laced with some form of narcotic. Ironically, this realization occurred after both of the burritos had been consumed by the four of us. It was at this point that Tyler and I gazed across the parking lot and saw a liquor store. Now now, none of us had any interest in alcohol, but what we were attracted to was another staple product of liquor stores: cigars. Tyler and I rushed over to the front door, waltzed in, and examined the selection. We settled on a peach, a grape, and a honey flavored cigar. The money was given to the kind foreign skinned brother behind the counter and we returned to the girls with good news in our hands. Or rather, good fumes.

Yeah,

that was the night we escaped the eventful parking lot with some scrapes on my car. The four of us decided that we required a memorable place to smoke the cigars. We ambled onward and came to the train bridge on the canal. This is the canal that divides Cape Cod from the rest of the world, and the elevated iron mammoth of a bridge residing over it. We parked in a dirt lot and walked to the stream. The stars hung so low their reflections dipped into the river and the blackness carried their light South. The cigars were ignited and TD demonstrated proper technique for smoking, then he smoked all three at once. Pictures were snapped and then some more pictures were captured. We all sat on a fence and broke the top bar. Then we took pictures of that.

Alas,

this was the night the cigars smoldered down to nothing and the butts were thrown into the brackish water. Due to our need for gazebo, we crossed the grass by the canal and tossed a football around in the darkness. A solitary lamp illuminated the entire park, making the ball hard to see, and therefore, difficult to catch. At this point, Natalie declared that she was going to sleep in the car because she had to work in the morning. Amanda answered with one of the best compliments I've ever received. She said, "you came with Ethan and you expected to *sleep?*" I laughed and thanked her immensely for the compliment. Sincerely.

Oh,

that was the night Natalie slept in the back seat of my car while Tyler, Amanda and I crossed the street to enter a bar. We walked in on the sound of a middle aged woman moaning karaoke and pool cues smashing the triangle. One of the men playing billiards had an amazingly long beard and smoked like a poet. We sat down at a table with dirty dishes on it, waited awkwardly for a few minutes, and walked out. The three of us returned to Natalie in the car, trying not to wake her, but we failed. So much life still resided in us.

And,

that was the night Natalie, Tyler, Amanda, and I drove home from the canal. I drove slowly enough to make the night last. I coined my term 'acoustic conversation' (*n. a quiet and contemplative discourse between a small number of individuals, often pertaining to the deeper aspects of life. Typically accompanied by melancholy roots music*). Music played just above the hum of the engine, allowing the three conscious occupants to fall head over heels into some deep conversation. We talked about love, about life, about our futures, about love again. Time was lost. Then a sign was posted on the side of the road: "Scenic Overlook Ahead." I slowed the car down and pulled over at the turn off. Amanda, TD, and I got out and tried to see what we could see, but in the blackness, we could not overlook much. There was simply a large rock on the side of the road which we climbed on, snapped pictures on, and laughed at. Due to Natalie's insistence on returning home to sleep, we got back in the car and headed on our way. Reluctantly, I drove to Amanda's house to return her home: a sweet gift on the front porch. It was a swift goodbye, with promise of a reunion the following day. Hope is always a good thing. Always.

I think,

that was the night Tyler and I drove to Natalie's front door to return her safely home. She said her groggy goodnights and the two of us departed to my house (or rather, the room I rented from an ancient French woman named Arlette who used to cook me French meals and pastries). Tyler and I could read each other. We read something beautiful that night. It was happiness, pure. The basest form of joy known to man. We drove to my rented room, ecstatic and energetic, despite the extremely late hour, and agreed that everything, yes everything, was right with the world at that moment. There was no fault to be found in it. That moment was ecstasy. We were on Route 28 when this moment occurred, passing by the White Hen Pantry.

Yah,

that was the night we returned back at the home I rented in Hyannisport. As we ascended the staircase, I was thinking about where TD should sleep. He piped up, "Well...it *is* a queen sized bed." I smiled big as a croissant and deemed it appropriate for us to share the bed. We got ready for sleep and went to bed, laughing and talking even later into the night. I wouldn't bet money on it, but we probably laughed ourselves to sleep that night. Then we woke up at six thirty the next day. So tired.

Yah,

that was the morning we agreed to meet Amanda at the racquetball court the next morning. We played some, but ended up lying on the the hardwood floors because we were so tired. I had to go to class, but Amanda and Tyler agreed to wait for me in the parking lot so we could skate after my lesson. The enthusiasm was lacking that of the night before. I reluctantly appeared to my class for twenty minutes, and when I returned to the vehicles, Amanda had gone home and Tyler was waiting for me to take him home. The morning after. The magic is never perfectly recreated.

Yah,

that day was now three years ago. I don't talk to Tyler or Natalie nearly as much as I should. Amanda pursued her dreams of the ocean and sailed away on a Navy ship. She never really came back, but her sweet salt water sustains her passion for freedom these days. As for me, I go to school in Chicago; a thousand too many miles from my home, the ocean. Few days rival the level of passion and life we each felt on Cinco de Mayo, 2010 now. Only the memory of the night can serve as magic enough for the evidence of life, the evidence of love, the evidence that some nights are worth living a lifetime for.

5/25/2010 al

Tell me when to stop
but don't ever say to go.
You don't teach kids how to sin
because they already know.
I'll hold your hand hard
on the mountain made of paint
I'd kiss the lips off of your face
if I knew you wouldn't faint.
Sister sacred, hike a hill
and turn into the sun.
I know I barely know you,
but I think we're nearly done
with being friends and nothing more,
with clogging up our pores.
With bleeding through our nostrils
and staying home from wars.

6/2/2010

Follow you to Philadelphia,
I'll follow you to Perth.
I'd love you on a mountainside
somewhere across the earth.

I'd love to see your windblown hair
dance spirals 'cross your face,
the same one that sings those songs
and songs of God's eternal grace.

Frisbee
6/18/2010

Sing loudly from the mountain as the sun sets on your shoulders,
and the rest of your body follows as you grow a little (c)older.
You'll dive into the grass, singing "clarity is mine"
until you're breathing dirt and realize that your team is still behind.
We're not Galatians from Galatia, or any other given book,
but we're known to come up short when for love is what we look.
Sing 'reddened thigh, oh me oh my,' you shall not conquer me;
but death in all his faces likes to burn my skin so softly.
And cancer takes a shovel and he digs himself a home
when I'm 'round the world exploring but I'm really all alone.
Is this what you've come to mean: you're an adventure wrapped in skin?
Or are you just pretending so we never will begin?
I told you in the airport that my like for you's sincere,
but since that day in West Palm, your rejection I have feared.
Now as I'm catching up to you in orbits 'round the sun,
please tell me that you mean it when you say I'm loads of fun.
Because clarity stings swiftly, and I've said this once before;
that what I thought were windows were really hardwood floors.

6/22/2010

Think: do I know anyone
quite like you?
Will there be others for me
elsewhere?
God,
please tell me
a) why she said that
and
b) why it hurts so much.
Of course you're long distance, dear;

you're a traveler.

The Hummingbird
6/29/2010

Find me elsewhere when I'm lost.
I'll meet you up here on the coast.
You'll tan your arms and gain some weight.
We'll gaze at stars and stay up late.
My hummingbird, you love the sweets,
so it's too bad they rot your teeth.

Find me right here when I'm found
and let me swing you round and round,
Sister, sing songs of the Cape.
Write poems to which I can't relate.
Yes, spill yourself all over me,
because after all, that's all I need.

India
10/30/2010

Some bumrushed roadside Indians
took in this paleskin lad.
They fed him rice until he popped
and went stark raving mad.

Some brown neck naked Indians
gave me some dirty drink.
I sucked it down till dead and dry,
I's far too sick to think.

Some sunburnt bird's eye Indian
did teach us how to work.
Yet when push shoved beneath the sun,
he turned into a jerk.

Some broad nosed gnostic Indians
once showed us how to pray.
With hands up high and body lost,
we do it every day.

I Wrote This On An Airplane
Fall, 2010

       Sister, let the lonely clouds
       tuck you softly in their path.
(You see) The ground is something islands eat—
       it makes the ocean laugh.
       In all your subtle wanderings,
       did ever once you see
       the youthful cloud whose father left;
       his mother set him free?
       So over oceans strangely calm
       he squanders all his days,
       just looking for some way to show
       his everlasting praise?
       Sister, this one lonely cloud,
       he'll never find his rest,
       but wanders in between the Blues
       still searching nonetheless.

Well, since the last days dripped with sweat
and home was nowhere near,
we've spent our hours licking up
this somewhat salty fear.
Yet well beyond these wasted months
is air again to breathe
and to inhale, sans stinging bugs,
we thought would never leave.

I wrote this to you Saturday
and mailed it Post Express.
I couldn't say where virtue went;
one word is like the next.
And chivalry…well it expired,
and sports cars took its place,
so all that man has left to do
is drive. And drive with grace.

I hoped you'd read it by today;
I see I hoped in vain.
So unfamiliar as it sounds,
just please let me explain.
In uniform, I broke the code;
the whole world suffers still.
And though you can't forgive me now,
I pray someday you will.

Arms rise, shrink and expand.
Heaven,
where are you?
Heaven, I have felt your pain,
what wakes you up,
wrapped loosely around my wrist.

Sister, sometimes what you sing
passes smoke-ringed lips.
Blow your holes in something
else.
Better yet,
blow no holes.

Not in science, not in love,
not in feelings from above,
not in airplanes or in books,
not in man's amazing looks.
Let me tell you about
tact.

There once was a princess
and her name was not
yours.
Nevertheless, we strive on,
one and all
for majestic dresses.

I'm 'boutta open up a big can of brutal honesty...

Nov. 27th, 2010 at 12:31 AM

Being lonely on Thanksgiving stinks. New Zealand is cool 'n' all, but family comes before scenery on my priorities.

I'm excited to be home for a season and recharge before I get the impulse to fuel up the car and head East again.

Southeast, to be specific.

- **Current Mood:** Distant

sneezing with my retainer in

Freedom.

I called Laura from the beach in Chatham. Natalie and Amanda waited patiently while we chatted away the time we'd lost. I told Laura we should drop by her work. She said she'd forgotten how free I was.

That night was incredible, and if you read this, Natalie, Amanda, or anyone else who was involved, you rule. No excuses. We painted black ribbons on the fresh blanket of snow that had fallen on the streets of Cape Cod. Tailed by the 5-0, we made a run for it to the bridge where there would be 24 hour food and a scenic overlook. The night was simple and elegant. Nothing is as beautiful as the feet that bring good news, and we took the good news of reunion all over that gorgeous peninsula. Of course there is the tearing at my gizzards, beckoning the reality that if I moved back there, it would not be nearly as magical as I imagine. I love the Cape, but it is now a winter house to me; a greenhouse where I go every so often to see how my flowers are doing, but I do not live there.

Now it's Colorado. Now big things happen regularly with this new line up of almost-as-epic people, but the tone is not matched. Nothing compares when you're in a landlocked state. I need my ocean, and I'll be there soon enough come February.

Your kingdom come…even in Colorado…

12/23/2010

Dear Amanda,
    Don't take this the wrong way, but you're beautiful.
    Something primal
    stirs beneath your blondish locks;
    something that lets the writers sing
    and poets weep.
    Sister, I'd drive you anywhere,
    knowing the Law is in pursuit.
    I'd swim for you,
    I'd swim to sea.
    I'd swim the sea.
    I'd swim to see
    you.

12/25/2010

Remind myself that life's happening now.
Sail the oceans, get to the coast somehow.
Regardless of dreams, I'm here in the conscious,
where I'm leaning on the oak and thinking of conches,
of diving off docks into the Pacific,
of flying the sail and then going with it.

See, this is where I'm lost,
where the separate paths have crossed.
Along one trail runs my story,
the adventure raw and gory.
Along the other runs my time,
never slowing down to rhyme.

So here is the facet,
the Christmas day tangent.
The thought has gone on and taken the wind.
It's flying a kite just around this next bend.
The question is chase, and the answer is yes,
say, let's seize this old map and go hunt for the X.

2011

THE YEAR I WAS STOKED

I returned home from YWAM with more frenetic energy than a girl with a bee in her bonnet. My jaunt across the continents changed the way I lived and *wanted* to live; it showed me that there is so much of the world I have left to see, and I had been living in such a tiny hermitage, and life could be so much more enormous.

Upon returning home to Colorado, I somehow slid into the role of volunteer youth pastor at a tiny church, where I fueled the students up with a similar amount of charismatic hype and fervency. I was still close enough to them in age that they were just as much friends as students, and several still are to this day.

I continued pursuing my Associates degree in writing at another community college, and did everything possible in my free time to make my life adventurous as possible. I was a rock climbing instructor and intentionally filled the rest of my time with things like flying Cessnas and riding horses. I became obsessed with sailing, which is a rough obsession if you're in Colorado.

That summer was a real shift though: Two friends and I decided to go on a missions trip to Brazil, but stay for two extra weeks in order to backpack around the country. To this day, those two weeks are some of the best of my life.

The missions trip was amazing by itself. I met a beautiful girl named Giovanna and we wrote each other songs with acoustic guitar accompaniment, and explored the decrepit town of Brodowski, which included an abandoned insane asylum which was rumored to be haunted. We would write each other letters after I returned to the States, but they would get rarer and rarer until they stopped altogether.

The trip to Rio was incredible as well. Starting from our friend Lucas' home in São Paulo, we set out to make it to Rio de Janiero by any means necessary. Lucas had a girl waiting for him there. He, Joel and I used ferries, local buses and the vehicle of anyone who would give us a lift. We also walked. A lot.

Perhaps the most memorable episode in Brazil happened in the coastal town of Paraty (pronounced PAD-a-CHI), a beautiful colonial village on a bay with 17th- and 18th-century buildings set atop cobblestone streets so bumpy no vehicles can enter the town.

Our hostel was right on the beach, and every night during happy hour, the beach bar served free Caipirinhas. That was the most concentrated shot of alcohol I had ever consumed at the time, so I took my shot while we were talking to a tall, fat Australian man named John. When I got up to walk back to the bar, the floor slid slightly diagonal.

I didn't like being tipsy (and still don't), so I decided that the best course of action was to take off running and exercise it out of my system. I intended to just trot over to the water and back, but once I reached the beach, I just kept going. Clad only in my swim trunks, I ran up the beach until I hit the river path. Then I ran that, barefoot, all the way to the edge of the town.

I came to an ancient Catholic church on the outskirts of Paraty and fell prostrate on its steps, expecting to have some gigantic spiritual epiphany. I didn't, so I ran the handful of miles back to our hostel. When I got back, Joel told me that when I ran off, Australian John watched me go and asked him, "So, uhh, is this gonna be a short thing or is 'e gonna be at it for a bit?" Joel just shrugged.

When we got to Rio, we got mugged at gunpoint on Copacabana.

Back in Colorado, I wrapped up my first college degree and continued peppering the vacant days with hikes and spontaneous drives of various sorts. I met a girl at a street ministry whom I tried to pursue for the next several months, but who would continually shoot holes in my attempts. For months, she hinted that it just wasn't the right time for her, until she finally got to the point where she told me that it would never be the right time—something she could have said months earlier...

1/6/2011

days pass without meaning
and a moon rises over water.

somewhere that i'm not
a boat puts out to sea.

o voyage, ye brave ones,
make me proud.

1/7/2011

some things, some expressions
painted on a holiday face,
are lost in pixels far too wide,
too blurred or sharp
and can't decide.

some people just have time to be
exactly who they try to be.

Anna,
1/22/2011

I've said it before
and I'll say it again:
I can try as I will,
but you're just not the one.

I wish that you were;
I wish it was so,
but I can't bring myself
to reverse let you go.

We can drive through the night,
you're asleep on my arm,
and I wish, oh I wish,
I could battle your charm.

It wraps 'round my head
and it wisps in my breath,
but I simply can't say
that I'll love ya till death.

strike with chaos

Mar. 27th, 2011 at 1:00 PM

Dave's not into beat poets like I am. Kerouac can make a heart come alive, and he certainly does mine. That night, we read deep into the enthusiasm of the beat generation, lying barefoot on the industrial strength carpet of Barnes & Noble. That, followed by Sun Tzu's *The Art of War* led to a not-too-awful night in Colorado.

We balanced across cables in the car park and hopped walls twice our height. We drove headlong into bushes, carried by shopping carts; slicing up our legs and faces. Dave got bush in his eye.

The MANlypics. This should be televised.

At least the videos are on Facebook.

• **Current Mood:** Manly

The Tie-Dye Hearse
4/26/2011

A white washed face and folded shirts,
he's nothing but a tie-dye hearse.
He'll hold your hand and kiss your cheek
and compliment your slim physique,
for on his mind are legs and busts;
he fills his head up with such lusts!
He'll bring you roses—daffodils,
and feed you chocolate just for thrills.

If you were me and I were you,
I'd ship myself off to Peru,
where indiscreetly, way down there,
I'd hide myself from his affairs.
Yes, he's no good like seeded grapes;
he'd prob'ly buy you ugly drapes!
I hope, my dear, that you won't see
that selfish man is really me.

5/5/2011

T-shirts till the sun rises,
then sleep.
Sister, pull me on like your tee.
there's something scientific about
chemistry.

See, in the silence after we hang up,
all I can hear is a ringing.

call again.
Call ahead.

Come Home.

5/5/2011

A year ago to date today,
we found ourselves a fifth of May,
so bold and soft and brightly hued,
we were not quite sure what to do.

We drove and drove and broke some laws.
We sucked down water, sans the straws.
A year ago to date today's
the best day ever, I must say.

We smoked cigars and put them out
in Cape's canal to burn the trout.
We tossed a football, couldn't see
the white gazebo, or skinny tree.

Now, one would want to sleep at night
and thinking so would prove quite right,
but as you said—you're never wrong—
if you want sleep, don't come along!

I'm Tired
Undated Poem, 2011

I'm tired of Christians who don't
know how good
our God is.

White Blood
6/9/2011

I fought like you never knew I could
now these hands you held are turning into wood
and you're losing the battle inside yourself
a weapon we use but we've never understood

let's beat it with stones till the record breaks
and throw up, sober up if your stomach aches
you're losing the battle inside yourself
so draw lots to determine which side to take

there's a white horse with white blood running out of me
he told me I'm free, like a Pharisee
and I'm losing the battle against myself
and I'll watch it unfold, but there's no way to foresee

See, I'm the air every king used to dictate
every word that was stolen from the laureate
when he lost every war he fought against himself
are you worried yet? are you worried yet?

so it seems that this arm is a counterfeit
these legs have been places I would never think
and this mouth runs just a bit too much
so it sleeps now to let my fingers speak

Hallelujah
6/21/2011

It's a Monday morning altar call with your face you painted red
and there's a voice inside saying put up a smile
though you think that God is dead,
but the fact remains that your dad's remains
have been heavy on your mind
so you close your eyes and you swallow that pride
and you hope that God is kind,

> It's the quietest hallelujah that you've ever heard
> and if you think that God is silent, He made you with a word
> crying, oh, my broken child just take this hand, take this hand

It's that Thursday evening fire alarm, you've slipped through the floor,
you say my family's in a different state, why live anymore?
but the fact remains that these earthly pains
have been heavy on your mind,
so you close your eyes and the pain subsides
and you hope that God is kind

> It's the weakest hallelujah that you've ever heard
> and if you think that God is weaker, He made you with a word
> crying, oh my broken child just take this hand

> It's the strongest hallelujah that you've ever sung
> and if you think that God is weak, well then you're just dead wrong
> singing, oh my God, my Father, just take this song, take this song

finally! score!

You know how sometimes you see a picture, a glimpse, or a video of someone and it just plain hurts?

There was this popping sound behind my left ear. They always say it's heartbreak, but be real: emotions drain from your brain, not the blood pumping muscle in your anterior cavity.

I saw her skin, wrapped comfortably around her skull—and the way her eyes read that book; forget the title, it's her eyes I was focused on. Those natural sloughs rooted beneath that pesky strand of hair that continually tries to drape her vision.

The sway of her shoulders as she walks away. Talk about a sight I've become all too accustomed to over the years.

It's not been since that night watching the snow pass in front of the beam of the lighthouse that I've been near her. That night that wrapped itself in a subzero gown and strolled around Chatham. The quietest all-night adventure of my life, it got what it deserved. It was muted and beautiful, yet confusing in its simplicity.

Now waves break in the background of her Hollywood life. See what another year gives her. Gives me.

Will she finally wake from her breezy amours into the arms of reality? Time tells and God knows…I'll find out.

I never say goodbyes. I say See You Laters.

Sometimes they feel about the same.

Lilley Hall

Jun. 29th, 2011 at 12:48 AM

I kissed you in my dream last night
and you apologized
for all the things you said before;
you hadn't realized
that way below the hemisphere
down on the Sunny Coast,
you'd met the man to call you his,
the one who loves you most.
So in my dream, your hand in mine,
you met my eyes and smiled,
said this is what the grown-ups miss,
let's stay like this a while.

Nell
7/3/2011 am

I don't know what the deal is, I don't know where to start
see I've barely just met you, yet your life is an art.
From painting to pieces of pottery pearls,
there's this fire inside you, igniter of girls.
It's this solid black ruby, so perfect and rare,
it's the beauty inside you from your toes to your hair.

And I'll never get to tell you,
and you may never know,
but if no one else tells you,
to me you're beautiful.

See, I've waited and waited and waited some more,
yet the finger's still naked, my heart's growing sore
from these girls and their daydreams, their love without time,
but I'll wait and I'll wait till the day that you're mine.
With some eyes wearing tree leaves with sun shining through,
the wind moves you gently, and it's moving me too.

And I may never tell you,
but my mouth is so full.
It needs to just say
that you are beautiful.

once a day

Jul. 5th, 2011 at 4:16 PM

Once a day I fall in love.
Be it her beauty, her smile,
or an innocent shrug
once a day I fall in love.

•   **Current Mood:** Pining

When I initially posted this brief couplet on my LiveJournal page, my friend Natalie commented something like, "Exactly. When you meet the right one, it will be the little things about her that keep you enthralled."

I replied to her that sadly, the intent of the post was not a cute ode to a current or even a potential lover, but it was much more depressing and less romantic. While Natalie read the poem as being only to one person, I meant it to be read with a constantly changing antecedent.

As a perpetually single bachelor for the majority of my life, I wrote this poem thinking about the fact that I seem to 'fall in love' with a different girl every day. One day, it may be the way this woman smiles. The next day, I may see another walking down the street and become enamored by her hair. And so on.

But I'm working on it, alright?

I Saw That Day In Sepia
7/24/2011 aa

I saw that day in sepia,
I heard you speak in rhyme.
I told you that there is none
when you asked me for the time.

I saw your face in porcelain,
the easy kind to break.
I tried to draw your figure on
an old Egyptian plate.

I took your picture in the grass,
your hands behind your head.
I tried to tell you, wait for love
you made your own instead.

I see the day in sepia,
you tell me you're now two;
a person lives within you now,
our time has passed on through.

I see your face in pictures now,
in black and white and green.
You're holding both your children near,
and holding in a scream.

Most days I don't wake up in New York,
but there are certainly days that I do.
I'll find myself caught in the haze of the gray
and I catch myself thinking of you.
Most days I'm not found in an airport,
where I wander around blowing time,
interpreting folks, aimless flipping through books,
and penning a cute little rhyme.
Most days I'm just up in the air,
about Denver and Long Island hair,
but I'll write to you when all the words in my pen
have grown restless and lay themselves bare.

———————

Recycled air, turned
over and ejected—Nostril,
lung, nostril. Here,
take these words,
one airplane to another:
I take what's inside
to my grave.

Patience
wearing thin,
patients
gaining weight.
One homophone to
another:
Let's see what
you're made of.

ourselves

Jul. 26th, 2011 at 12:03 AM ag

Let's not write about ourselves. Let's not riddle the web full of holes demanding attention and ranting about our lives. I know we all think this, but who lives it?

Certainly not I. Certainly not I.

Why should I jot down another hasty entry about some brown eyed beauty I've met in Brasil? What would keep me from penning my reasons for why she is captivating the majority of my thoughts as of late? Is it wrong to continue to pepper the public with these pining ideals and whimsical entries? Maybe it's that white t-shirt she wore draped loosely over her frame. Perhaps it was the song she wrote me the day before we split. Above most else, though, I think it was the way she danced to the constant soundtrack of her mind.

Her prayers both heartfelt and terse lifted up a woman's soul. She lay her life bare upon her knees, with her hands folded on the cheap plastic chair.

It's the spirit inside her that makes me sing.
It's the Spirit inside her that makes me long.

Hours of silence and prayer await me in the coming days. But once again, why would I bother y'all with that nonsense?

- **Current Mood:** Awake
- **Current Music:** Something Jazzy

Brazil, It Is A Poem
Summer, 2011 ag

Lady, put your things by mine. We're on the first bus to Rio
Lady, do you have the time? Anything to talk to you
Black ribbon sleeping in your hair; art textbook resting in your lap
Smell your perfume floating through the air, from the lotion you put on
your hands

    (Chorus)
When this beach led to favela, I couldn't find the words to tell ya,
There's no space between these homes.
Where there's no concrete on the roads, I had to write to let you know,
Brazil, it is a poem (Brazil is just a poem)

A thief who never made a kill, is just a child in the bright sunshine
He's begging for a softer will, down to his last bottle of wine
Sister fell asleep on the bus, slowed breathing dripping from her lips
Sister take a picture with us, we'll leave each other with a kiss

    (Chorus)

Darlin', you're still on my mind, a dancer in my constant head
Darlin', they say love is blind, it should have covered up my mouth instead
Cause I keep writing songs to you, when every neuron in my head says stop
But you're adventure in a girl costume, Brazilian artist in a plain white top

    (Chorus)

So sing it out!
For every girl who ever touched a globe,
Sing it out!
To every boy who's ever hopped a boat,
Sing it out!
I think you're missing what I'm saying here,
Sing it out!
Because we're bored and we're not staying here.

30 days: day 1
Aug. 7th, 2011 at 3:12 AM

So I have decided to do one of these photo challenges. Mainly to be honest, and not care what people think, but to honestly express some things I like, regardless of what society or other people say of them. SO…

Day 1: A Photo of yourself with 15 facts.

1. It didn't necessarily say 15 facts about me.
2. I will always choose summer over winter and ocean over mountains.
3. Favorite band ever: Bright Eyes.
4. I wear a retainer every other night.
5. Bunny rabbits cannot vomit. Nor can horses.
6. I miss Cape Cod so much, yet think that if I moved back there now, it would not be how I imagine it.
7. I love talking about my dreams.
8. I often wish I were still in high school. Time moves too fast.
9. You can never have too much sky.
10. I'm terrified of tornadoes.
11. God should always be getting bigger in your mind.
12. I can't sit still for too long. Even when I relax, I need to do something.
13. Rain is cool.
14. I often think about doing more YWAM.
15. If I meet my wife this year, it'll be nuts because I got a sign from God earlier in the year.

Hey G,

This will probably not be the first letter I ever send you, but I hope you do read it sometime. You see, the Romans did not judge a man's life by what he did when he was alive. Instead, when a man died, they placed one question over him: Did he have <u>passion?</u>

I don't know if I'll ever put my finger on it, but in those first few hours I know you, I saw just that: passion. I love the fact that you dance without ceasing to some hidden rhythm of your heart. Words cannot express how my soul is moved by the grace in the movement of a dancing girl. I have always wished I could dance like that, but these bones simply will not allow it. I have simply decided to be content in observing, and hopefully, in meeting a girl as graceful as you.

About a year and a half ago, I had one of the most impactful dreams of my whole life. I was sailing around the world, and in the early evening of some dusky, exotic country, we approached a dock. The sky was golden orange beyond the land, and it silhouetted a figure on the dock. She was a beautiful exotic girl, standing on the edge of the sea waiting for the ships to come in. I stepped off the ship and shook her hand.

"I'm Ethan," I said. "Want to come around the world with me?"

She said yes without hesitating and stepped on board.

Ever since I woke up that morning, I've been searching for that exotic beauty to sail around the world with me, whether literally or figuratively. It seems as if I fall in love with a new girl every day, but since we split at the end of my trip, I haven't been able to shake you from my head. I've begun to wonder if maybe—just maybe—you are that girl from the dock. I wonder if you could be her.

(unfinished)

Fall, 2011?

(These little undated poems were found on a loose piece of pocket notebook paper after ordering the original proof for this book. The date is based on who they're addressed to.)

So full of passion, full of soul,
you're full of tears and bullet holes.
O Giovanna, tempt me not,
you've taken captive every thought
and laid it bare like aftermath,
you're my beloved mustard gas
in times of war, and when it's still,
I picture you by window sills
where all good summers go to die
and lovers fade like setting skies.
It's here you weep in shades of green;
it's here your movement sets me free.
You dance to rhythms soft as rain
that stir your legs to this refrain.

(on back of small paper:)

In Paraty, a Catholic church,
a hostel and a bar
On Koh Samed, a sailor's tomb,
some women and a scar.

And here in Denver, winter's home,
some dusted willow brush
and in your chest, a weighted line,
the one thing I can't touch

Fall, 2011? am
*After ordering the proof for this book, I was going through some old papers in
a drawer of my childhood desk and found even more poems scrawled on loose
sheets of paper. This one was written down a giant white napkin, surprisingly
without a single word crossed out or rewritten. I do not remember writing it, or
when exactly, but based on who it's addressed to, Fall 2011 is my best guess.*

In every single hair of mine
resides a thought of you—
they hold my passion, sans the thought
of ever changing hue.
You see, this repartee of ours
has morphed into a stone
concrete and ever tangible,
we should not be left alone.
For loneliness, like apple seeds,
must die before they bloom
and seeing eyes as dark as yours,
you've clearly left the womb.
And fingers curled to wipe an eye—
an eye as dry as mine—
you'll find that there is little
that is left to make me cry.
But Molly, dear, you know by now,
you know that we must move
into a place of wisdom,
not into a fear to lose.
And fear of men and fear alone
stands now in our offense,
and should commence more passion still,
you'll readily convince
this sweatered schlub, this tattered man,
this boy without a clue,
that all he really needs in life
is God and bread and you.
So when at last this listless hand
extends to fasten yours,

do not retreat or pull away—
for we belong outdoors,
running, screaming, spooking deer,
we'll celebrate the green;
freshness of leaves, of sand and sea,
and all that lies between.
So hasten now, and do not fear
this open-hearted door,
for all I want—no, all I need's—
to make this castle yours.

Marissa
8/19/2011 am

You were a picture that I drew in May,
of a ship anchored calmly in Bennington Bay.
You were that poem that stirred me inside,
about climbing up trees and the last time you cried.

You became postcards from further away
with occasional rips and the edges all frayed.
You were a toy with a velveteen soul,
stripped down until nothing could make you feel whole.

You were that girl who I kissed in July
in the woods as the fireworks rained from the sky.
You are the ice creamy drip down my cone,
filled with chocolaty terror of being alone.

And now you're a poem, lines taken apart.
A Japanese brushstroke without any heart.
And I had forgotten the mark I had made
until that night in August, your soul was displayed.

10/11/2011

Sit behind your telescope and stare into the galaxy,
you can see a crystal ant who's always staring back at me.
The homeless wander aimlessly across a busy street
while the rich man wanders aimlessly with better looking teeth.
I see your point in pointing dear, now put the fist away.
There's nothing left for you to hit but words I've left to say.
Take these bones you've claimed as yours and bring them back to life,
I want to see a miracle, not wait to live my faith.
In courtesy we've drawn a line; we've humbled out our bounds,
yet crossing them has proven wrong, as your sobs and tears abound.

My Father works out on Cape Cod, He uses me the most
for reaching kids with sand filled shoes; I must be by my coast.

Potential
11/18/2011

I wish I could fill up a dirty glass of water
until it overflowed and cleaned its own exterior;
stains wash away and beautify crystal.
Can you see me when I stand opposite you?

Hole in my pocket,
these thoughts are spilling through.
Love it when you stop in
we'll spill away the afternoon.

11/27/2011

My calmest state is winter
'cause I live there after fall.
I'm quiet and complacent, for
my home's here after all.

Lord, let me not forget about
the me I'd like to be.
The artist lip-locked summer breeze
who's jogging by the sea.

I'd gift wrap my identity
and open it on Christmas day,
in tearing back the wrapping job
I'd receive what I'd prayed.

In summer I don't have this urge
to go and self-create,
because I'm often somewhere else,
quite lost and swimming late.

Yet now that days bereft of heat
have come and taken residence,
I find myself in need of warmth;
this drive has taken precedence.

At four a.m., or afternoon,
I look for sunrise colors bare
as poetry upon the page,
or music drifting in the air.

I know I knew these hues one time;
I know I will again,
but till that time when life meets art,
I'll fake it with my pen.

A Song for Nell
12/14/2011 am

Sunset doll you're effervescent,
glowing near the ground.
To touch your skin, it's heaven's best,
I see my fingers drown.

Sunrise soul, I've seen you run,
I've seen your painted walls.
And to this weakness, I give in,
to your morning wake-up calls.

And to this end, I've worked so hard,
I've waited there for months,
but long forgot and two for two,
we're bound to have some fun.

So you and me, like binary—
the code we used to speak,
the ones and o's the bucks and does,
the love of these two geeks—

are painted on some canvas sheets,
a dress to clothe the sky,
but lost within a fireside,
we'll never have to die.

Oh thank you, thank you, thanks again,
I'm glad that we could talk.
But should commence a second chance,
I'd blow like powdered chalk.

And should you feel the same as me,
or should you feel alone,
just know that you, by far, are my
eternal skipping stone

A kiss! To kiss! To bind our lips,
to bind our lips as one!
To sail the seas! To walk the beach!
To beat on Ginsberg's drum!

To fly! To soar! Release balloons,
And never see them land!
In glory we, like glorious trees,
have diamonds on our hands!

Re: Nell
12/15/2011 am

It is for fear that the other may evaporate in your absence that you delay bidding goodnight to a loved one. It is the reason time becomes light and travels as such when that person is near, and yet, in the midst of it, you cannot seem to soak in enough of the other's presence to be satisfied for some time. They are your water; your oxygen. Bleeding is just annoying if they are not red. Nell, it would be nice to have you on the other side of my skull, but since you're in there, make yourself at home. Fix some supper and call me Captain. And please, Darlin', don't evaporate.

12/21/2011

How much of you do you give away?

The falling snow says shhhh to the world
and the drivers on the streets share a sense of camaraderie
from the softness of the roads.

The Darkest Eyes You've Ever Seen
12/31/2011 am

Capo 2
C Am F G
C Em Csus4 G

Yes, they're
the darkest eyes you've ever seen
I've been
looking for a way to see you, here

Captain,
your ship is scared to sail the sea
I see
a much bigger storm that's approaching

    (Chorus)
    All you see is
    part of me and
    all I want is
    all of you

Your kite
is a blue and black epiphany
Your teeth
form a question that I cannot answer

This map
forces us the long way home
Sunrise
and I am only driving away from (you)

    (Chorus)

In the Winter
Winter, 2011

Inside the houses, ghosts regard the bay with empty eyes.
From empty docks and empty boats, the phantoms start to sigh.
They exhale silence, move the waters—curtains in the breeze,
and with each swell, the quiet curls, the ghosts slip out to sea.

The summer homes sit still as stone, a throne without a queen,
and time to time, with vigil kept, a scamper can be seen.
Some movement here, a rustle there, a child's hand escapes,
and anything you thought you saw has drifted with the wake.

2012

HOMELESS AND HAPPY

One of the funnest years of my life was 2012.

I think I was on a total of 28 flights.

I began the year by blindly moving to Boston to volunteer with the YWAM base out there, and it was a whirlwind from day 1. I arrived at the base—a huge 19th century funeral home which was beautiful but falling apart—and the staff showed me my bunkbed and dresser where I could unpack and move in. I emptied my duffel bag and backpack into it, then headed down to the second floor to become better acquainted with the students.

Not two hours after I finished unpacking, an all-base meeting was called by the base director who told us he had just finished showing the fire marshal around the building.

It was condemned.

We had 24 hours to move out, and could not live there anymore until construction was completed. However, rather than being discouraged by this news like normal human beings, the YWAM kids and I were ecstatic. We were excited to be homelessly bouncing around from place to place for the next couple months, never quite knowing where we would be laying our heads at night.

Around that same time, a friend of mine from YWAM Denver called me to ask if I would help him out with a project he was starting in Nigeria. I told him I'd think about it for a week and get back to him. A week later, I called and told him I was in.

"Great!" he said. "You're the co-president!"

I was shocked. Never before had I been the co-anything of anything, much less even been to Africa. But I accepted and made plans to fly to Nigeria in April. When I called Mommy to tell her I was going to Nigeria in two months, her immediate response was, "Well hopefully the population of Nigeria doesn't get kicked out when you arrive so you'll be homeless there too."

& & &

When I look back on 2012, it feels like so much happened that it's hard to believe it all fit into one year. In order to fly to Nigeria, I had to hitchhike from Boston to NYC to meet up with my friend and catch our flight. This meant passing through many sketchy towns in Connecticut and witnessing many shady things on my voyage through.

After the first trip to Nigeria where we met our contacts and made connections, I decided to move back to Cape Cod for the summer because a friend of mine owns a surf shop and asked me to be his Stand-Up Paddleboard instructor. I said of course.

"Where will you live?" he asked me.

"I don't know, on the beach?" I said.

And I did.

The other employees were baffled by this homeless-looking beach bum who occasionally took trips to Nigeria for a few days "just for meetings."

That summer I also made some dear life-long friends who let me crash on their couches more times than I can remember. We would take the occasional spontaneous road trip down to New York City just to get Shake Shack burgers or hear Tim Keller preach. I spent most of my time sitting on the beach in the sun or paddling around on the ocean, so by August, my skin was as dark as my hair. Sand and salt were irreversibly embedded in my body and I loved it.

That's why it was such a jarring shift to fly to Chicago straight out of this season and into the rigid, formal, conservative campus of Moody

Bible Institute. The routine seemed to heave sand into my gears and I threatened to leave on more than one occasion (per week).

By the end of the first semester, I had adjusted to college life and began to dive deeper into the Word of God than I ever had before. I also began to date an old high school friend...

I wrote her a poem on a napkin

Jan. 2nd, 2012 at 2:40 AM

I wrote her a poem on a napkin, but this isn't it.
I tried to think of the best way
to convey
the joy of today;
the 8.5 hours I spent with you,
not not enjoying a second of it.

I wrote you a love poem on a napkin, or should I say,
a song of earnest yearning.

- **Current Mood:** Chipper
- **Current Music:** Stone Walls

Declaration
1/4/2012

You're free
and I'm free,
so let's be free together.

1/13/2012

You are an infomercial.
I think I've got you down,
think I've got you all figured out.

But wait, there's more...

147

1/19/2012

You're the breadth of a clothespin
and the breath of a sparrow,
you're the string the boy holds onto
when he restrains my flying eros,
you're the stroke of an artist
and the thief of his painting,
you're a mountain in the desert
when my arid heart is aching.

You're the song of the sailor,
the dance of the kite;
you're the one and only human
to ever make me feel so light.
You're as perplexing as a labyrinth
that the old Egyptians made
and if you ever find your way out,
come and find me in the shade.

1/21/2012

let's just travel,
let's just go
no destinations,
need to know.
let's just drive
let's hit the road,
we'll buy some food
and throw a load.
don't stop here, no
time to blow,
just rubber wheels
and open roads.

Waiting
1/29/2012

Silently I'm sinking to the bottom of the sea.
Underwater you don't bleed, just sink until you're free.

You are an enigma with a soft and fragile smile.
I'm worried 'cause I haven't seen it for a while.

And I am gonna wait for you, my kite without a string
'cause all these miles 'way from you amount to not a thing.
In this pursuit, the waiting proves the battle for your heart.
So swimming 'cross the ocean is a meager, wanting start.

I have no other option than to yield my yearning soul,
to ask your Father for you and to walk until I'm whole.

Leaving you is easy, it's the coming back that's hard,
'cause silently I watched you with a telescopic heart.

Spring, 2012

She picks me up like a crane
with her strong arms;
more legroom, please—she comes and goes
she comes and goes,
she flies away from me.
Now keep your eyes to the sky.

Wedding photos, wedding photographs
nothing trapped is nothing but the past

She flies away, she flies away from me
I didn't mean to, didn't mean to be strong

Skin upon skin,
but you're only ever touching
your own.

A life is just a memory made

I've lived a moment, watched it die,
I've seen it walk away—
or was it me, dear Memory,
who found it hard to stay?
'Cause looking back through clear repose,
I see in perfect light
a time bereft of end or flaw
the stars without the night.
With this revealed, I clearly see
the hollow chest in me—
the sunrise pit stop—transport van,
the disobeyed decree.
Yet holiness, this wholesome bliss,
this search within my veins
has led to only mountaintops
with cameras at the reins.

she said I think I'll go to Boston...

Feb. 29th, 2012 at 1:14 PM

Boston is awesome. Being homeless is great.
I'm well on my way to being okay.
I'm almost over you, yah, I'm almost to the place
where I can let this go to waste.
So write me a piece of literature,
and let me sing you songs
for under shooting stars you'll see
we were both a little wrong.

I'm on my way to forgetting you,
or at least how great we were
while standing on a mountaintop,
or taking racial slurs.
But now this longish winter has
begun to crack and peel,
and breaking through with sunlight beams:
the Bible's scroll and seal.

- **Current Location:** BOS

- **Current Mood:** Good
- **Current Music:** Party

The empty streets where children walked
and parents went astray
were swept and darkened far before
the end of every day.
And silence like a thief moves in,
descending on the streets.
And from a window's lofty view,
a song in dark repeats:

"Let go of your fences, let go of your land,
just go to the dances and take a lad's hand.
You've not got to lead him, you've just got to close
those eyes that are beads set on top of your nose.
He'll swing you and ring you and sing you a song
about lasses and lads who have swallowed their tongue.
She's got eyes like a fire, a grin like a crook
and she'll rob your desire, white wash every book.
She speaks telephoned words which the ear can't deny.
In a song like a bird, she'll repeat every line,
until broken and banished, alone and undone,
you'll realize she vanished; you'd never begun."

And slowly on and on it goes—
the chorus of the night,
until one day in bed I'll find
what's broken was made right.

Song for Sarah
4/9/2012 ak

A little bird came in my window
I kissed it on the lips and let it go.
You're the little bird in my window
I kissed you on the lips and let you go.

Pardon me as I let you know
you're all I want with that velvet soul.
Pardon me as I let you know
that I loved you then, we were white as snow.

A little song came through the air.
I danced a little bit though an old man stared.
I turned it up and we walked away
where we were all alone, out of his gaze.

You let me kiss you on the lips
you laugh at every joke I tell.
You're the only one of your kind, my
Sarah Bell.

4/10/2012 ak

The Starbucks kiss
that bound our lips,
it held us up like hands
to starry skies;
the How's and Why's
will never understand

what two old friends,
when one night ends,
will dare the other do,
but now it's past,
we dare not ask—
I'm glad that it was you.

From NYC
April, 2012 ak

I wrote you a simple poem
on the back of sermon notes
as I sat beside the Hudson
watching passing ships and boats.
This poem was more honest, see,
than those I'd penned before,
because I'd traveled NYC
until my feet were sore.
For in these travels, past few days,
I've hung with city girls.
I've seen my God do crazy things
and rock this city's world.
I've seen and done and drank some things
that change a grown man's life,
and seeing as I kissed you once,
I wrote my future wife,
saying nothing is so simple
when you come down from the hill.
So I wrote a simple poem
just to tell you how I feel.

Nigeria
April, 2012
Capo 6

Em	C	D	G

Sister, the softest skin is the patch that you lost in my kitchen.
Nigerian skin, the touch of your lips as I think till the morning.
Mother, the saddest eyes are the ones that you cast on the trav'ler,
Wandering to and fro, where the flesh it is fastened much tighter.
Cheap medicine, a Brazilian girl that I once was in love with,
tears on the sleeve of the coat that you left in the basement apartment.
I thought of you twice as I sat in the midst of the African diner.
My dad told me once, every boy, though he seeks,
      doesn't make him a finder.
Search till you're old, never found gold, and you weep long as winter.
Try as you may, every day you'll just wish that somehow you were with her.

My friend, I remember your face as the sun made a cradle before you.
I watched as you drank in the parking lot,
      laughed as the sugar controlled you.
Now do you remember the day we were blinded like love in the front seat?
A vie to impress, I feared that one day you would somehow forget me.

Well fears can grow wings, taking to flight in the form of an airplane.
And distance is kind, swallowing up every fragment of our pain.

You're My Home
4/12/2012 ak

Capo 4
C Cmaj9 Am G

Well baby I've been thinking lately
of all the things I should have kept,
and if you're gonna fly, fly straight
cause you're the one thing I have left.
Well do I make you weak in the knees now,
Cause darlin', you've the strongest eyes.
Or should I be looking at your shoulders,
just praying that you will not fly?

    (Chorus)
    You're my home
    Where I run to
    I'm coming home
    running to you (back to you)

Well I got tired of carrying this cross
and I don't think I'll make it alone
'cause I've been traveling all of this earth
and what I found is you're my home.
And I've got two empty hands waiting,
and I've still got a couple of bones,
no one's eyes burn me like yours do
so I'm still gonna call your arms home.

    (Chorus)

Well everything else is broken,
everyone else has all gone
and are you gonna join them too, dear,
or is your love really that strong?
Did you kiss me just as a friend then,
or was there something deeper too?
When everyone else is a liar,
I know you're my one that's true.

(Chorus x2)

Later Spring, 2012

I don't know what you did or who you crossed,
but it should be illegal to have skin that soft.
And it doesn't matter if I wait nine years
'cause time and space—yes, everything—has gone and disappeared.

The passion of a traveler's soul,
the beauty of the seas;
the two have shared a kiss so bold
it weakens sinners' knees.

4/13/2012

This road is alone
despite the cars on its spine.
To some it is home
and it may just be mine.

Because I'm on it alone
on the Peter Pan line
with a bus full of people
and a girl on my mind.

These smokestacks are ghosts
reaching up for the sky,
and the state line is close;
I left Boston behind.

From a bus full of strangers
with the young morning shine,
we'll sing Away In a Manger
and we'll lose track of time.

Because something is born
this Connecticut day,
conceived in a kiss
we shared miles away

in a state that's so dry
I've forgotten its name
over long days spent pining
for sweet ocean spray.

And I sang when I found it,
ran over the sand
just to realize that home
is the shell in my hand.

It can fit on my back
and it goes where I am.
So if you'll be my shelter,
then I'll be your man.

4/16/2012 ak

Sister, hold your head up,
you're more stable than you think.
All those broken flower petals
shouldn't tell you how to speak.

See, we bonded on the subway
and you told me how you fell,
how the flesh you cut the deepest
just continues not to heal.

So I gathered up my wisdom
and I gave you my advice—
just to close your eyes and exhale
as you're booking all these flights.

The air is thinner airborne
and that makes it hard to breathe.
So you whispered out some prayerful words
and told me you felt clean.

There is no word that I could pen,
no sentence I could speak
to tell you how a human being
changes in a week.

I'm not a different person now,
but these aren't the lips you kissed.
I wish I could explain somehow
but something would be missed.
I found that there exist no words
in any native tongue
to adequately capture me,
or you, or anyone.

See, people change. They misbehave.
They're old until they die.
But in their youth, they're mostly blind—
they see without their eyes.
I've spent my life pursuing things
that everyone can see,
but sometime in the last six days,
your eyes have opened me.

It's just this itching of discomfort that calls me by name—names me. The lusty trains of wanderloss have beckoned me to the loss of all that I know in homes and online. Here, there are no codes or formulas. Rather, there is a presence of lives guided only by emotion and desire—driven only by this madness to dwell in the state of passionate searching.

Have you found this plateau?

The peak is named Travel and the ascent is called Departure [from home].

In this, the season of motion, few things are longed for that can be gathered, accumulated or touched. These pinings are replaced, rather, with a collection of memories; with a desire to be touched, to be beaten out of sleep for trespassing; and to be with people. With someone to accompany you on this sojourn—to hear your thoughts and to share hers as you sit on the [surprisingly clean] stone floor of the bus terminal.

When I rid myself of the internet, of security, and of all I own, save a handful of backpack essentials, I gain the freedom of the open road and the liveliness that accompanies a commercial-free life.

Every woman becomes just that much more beautiful; every man that much more accommodating. The color in the sky and the cool wince of my skin under the rain is magnified exponentially. Ripples of a passing river offer comfort while before they would have been overlooked. And where in all of these glimpses of thriving life does God fit?

Everywhere.

Every raindrop to touch skin is an envelope of His love—a reminder that He hasn't forgotten you. I may weary of manmade dramas and what the world tells me my life should look like, but I believe that to seek Him is to travel, to violently escape comfort and find solace in omnipresent companionship. In this relationship, and in this relationship alone can I share my thoughts with someone who never tires of hearing them; and I can seek His perfect wisdom any time a Bible can be found or a prayer can be muttered.

One of the beauties of His Word is that I can read it in Brazil and it is just as true and accessible as in Boston; in Nigeria as in North Carolina.

My advice to you, dear readers, is to get out and find this discomfort. Get out and discover the joy of full reliance on YHWH.

5/1/2012
(Some things scribbled out, all on the same page)

Sing to signal search lights
I've been stranded in a sound.
There seem to be no pillow fights
when no feathers can be found.

—————

And this shower squeezes the New York cold
right out of me—
stranded in a sound,
sing to signal search lights
to find my absent acquaintances.
I met a girl on a crosswalk
and watched as she bit her nails;
her mind collided with a photo of herself
I took.

A special scent of solitude,
a weapon in your midst.
You've spent your life becoming things
the airplanes never kissed.
So let your skin show gratitude
and smile in your sleep,
for every song which dreams produce
is far too sweet to keep.

Place Your Hope in Summer, Son
Summer, 2012

Place your hope in summer, son; it surely shall return.
And rest ye not in women, for, they only fuel the burn.
Your counterfeit transactions land you halfway in the grave,
so place your hope in summer, it's where God spends most His days.

Delight yourself in weightlessness found 'neath the ocean's spray,
or rest your knees by kindred souls' to watch the ending day.
Go have that summer, soaked with her, those grinning suntanned eyes.
And when she smiles, kiss her head, you might just be surprised.

I've got my money, both my bills, on summer's victory
'cause when you have it, oh my son, run fast and come tell me.
Your eyes will stain your brackish cheeks with grief and joy the same;
the corners of your lips will dimple at the sounding of her name.

That skin you wear will bear the marks of rocks, bare feet, and sun.
And woe to me, I know the way it ends before begun.
So place your hope in summer, son, she will not let you down.
Just dive right in, don't hesitate. My son, I hope you drown.

Conglomerate
6/23/2012

Four years slowly, I've washed it all down
with some green and blue landscapes and a plane on the ground.
I got out of the Midwest and into the sea
and into that longing I never foresee.
I miss you so badly, I looked for you here,
but what do I owe you—or what do you fear?
You're a cold water call to a sailor's blue soul;
I'm a brake pad that's screaming. I'm punk rock 'n' roll.

Sister kiss me softly, see, this season is warm.
Sister, kiss me gently because you're stronger than her.

I see an empty wine glass and a heart full of pain,
I see a sunset rising over yesterday's rain.
I've seen a lonely night stroll the center of Times Square
I've seen you mouth goodbye through all the smoke infested air.
You sat beneath the stars and then I read you all my books,
but don't forget the reason that we baited all these hooks.
Our hearts intended death, but we've drawn a line before.
The only reason we're still here is Yahweh, living Lord.
I've seen a sunset fleeing water;
I watched a road grow black.
I've seen where we hid all the laughter
as we took the long way back.

7/17/2012

It isn't beautiful when the face
of hers filters through the window
and onto your screens.

It isn't beautiful when flatness overwhelming
rests on the sea
and starts to scream.

It isn't beautiful rising alone
beneath the stars of the day
and hitting the surf,

when all that you wanted
and all of you thinks
of God and a passionate girl.

It isn't beautiful to see her face
in the night
and to write her a song about love,

to long for her smile
to rest upon yours in a kiss
sealed in innocent blood.

It isn't beautiful when I think about me
and the mine
that I long to possess,

but someday this soul will be bored
with that blonde
picking daisies in last year's sundress.

It isn't beautiful when this late at night,
I find myself closing
my eyes to the song of her lips

and pining for greetings of some distant morn
when
my breakfast is served with a kiss.

NY, NY
7/1/2012
(Dictated to Bita while driving back to Cape Cod from NYC)

The models walk these ancient blocks
that cause the wise men rue.
The equator, the equinox,
will rot the whole world through.
Your tiny smile, our little talks,
the parade on which you rained
invited me, the idol walks
and laughs at what I've gained.

These bullet points and burger joints
both saw it from afar,
but toll booth fare, two bronzed coins,
grant passage to our car.
So rain did come, it misbehaved,
it stirred the sleeping girl.
It washes some and few get saved,
the rest just leave the world.

7/16/2012

You're the anchor of choice, delightfully strong.
You're the finest tuned string in a passionate song.
Now love me, Lord, lead me wherever You go.
I'll follow You blindly through sun and through snow.
Now there's a sea at my feet and a girl on my mind
and I'm panting for breath but I'm still far behind.
You're a rock and the center my life spins around.
You've shown me new places, no feet on the ground.
Some passion will spill and dissolve in the salt,
some tension will crumble and deepen the fault.
My God is a warrior, the Lord is His name,
and He's seeking His Church, His bride to reclaim.
And I'm seeking this girl like the waves hunt for sand
and I'm measuring breath and the smell of the land.
I pray to my God for this one to be true,
like the spin of the earth as it shrinks beneath you.
The fishermen know it, and so do the priests:
to travel the world is on what the soul feasts.
Enlightened to teach, like a girl skipping stones,
the desire to shrink is the marrow of bones—
to shrink not oneself, or the measure of legs,
but reducing the earth on this side of the lens.
The more places I see, the more places I've been,
and I'm chasing you, Jesus, though weary within.
The earth will give way, and the sky fall apart,
but from passion to passion, You've stolen my heart.

7/17/2012

I remember writing this on an airplane after watching a film in which the protagonist's father is killed in a mining accident. It's a quick flashback of a scene where he and his coworkers descend the mining elevator with chilling blank faces. It's such a minor clip in the film, but it stood out to me because of the eeriness of their faces. It's literally like a three second shot. I have no idea what film it was though, so if you know what I'm talking about can you please let me know? Thanks.

Twelve men descending
      down into the depths
Twelve men descending
      down into their deaths
Twelve men descending,
      their eyes straight ahead
Twelve men realizing
      they're better off dead
Twelve men tomorrow
      will sing in their sleep
With their blank faces sinking
      down into the deep.

7/31/2012 ab

I'm writing you a poem 'cause you're just too darn cute,
not because you asked me or you knit my parachute.
Your eyes have softened men before, and I am not the last.
Your pupils lead one deeper, through your Venezuelan past.
Oh, where have all the whistlers gone, the singers of your songs??
They heralded your melodies all day and all night long.
Your dresses are of velvet, crafted perfectly for you.
Your hair in darkness downward falls across your shoulders, two.

I'm writing you this poem as a new and dear, dear friend,
I see you as a beauty which a summer cannot end.
Your heart is set on fire, yet your eyes will put it out,
you'd better not look down or else the world will be without
your depth of soul and pretty face, extinguishing your spark.
The tears would flood these rusty shores and I would build an ark.
I'd sail away, alone with you, the bringer of the rain,
and together we would venture on, to Perth, Niger or Spain.

22 Airplanes
8/2/2012

Fly me over Africa, what good'll that do?
I know that You're changing me on flight 22.
22 airplanes in less than a year.
22 airplanes. I can't disappear.
I've written and slept over 44 wings
and I've inhaled locations you've seen in your dreams.
I'm the red-handed pilot, caught hopping around,
a poltergeist table, no feet on the ground.
I've been bumrushed and bankrolled. I've prayed like a saint.
I've often been absent when neighbors are faint.
This echoing longing for traveling love
is a light in the heavens, it's so far above.
So look up in evening for that blinking red light,
and blow kisses to Ethan, his 23rd flight.

8/2/2012

Man, go! Fly! Move! Burn!
<u>Verb</u> yourself and get.
Life is motion—God spoke it and it goes
goes
goes.
To fight it is rebellion—
let the wind take you and **move!**
Man, who are you to reject motion?
To reject change?
Life is changing, open your fists!
Life is movement, get on your boots!
Burn. Move. Fly. Go.
Please, my friend—
verb!

Paris Snaps
8/4/2012

I wrote these quick snippets about a trip to Nigeria and France on one of the flights back to Cape Cod. It was only a 5 day trip, so there wasn't enough content for a full recap, or even a satisfying journal entry, so I decided to condense the trip into this fun format of tweet-length vignettes.

He got up to help me stuff my duffel into the overhead compartment and I saw his height. His head towered three stories above his feet. I told him I know some Chinese people who have nightmares about legs that long. He told me he wrestles with leg room.

The phone rang and before he even answered, Izzy told me it was for me. I heard him answer with a groggy hello and then he hung up. I knew I had to put my feet on the floor and walk to the next room of the hotel. It was early. Unchristianly early. I knocked on her door and she answered in work out clothes. We did some crunches.

The van drove by full of boys my own age who had known nothing but Nigerian heat all their lives. They shouted *oyibo* at me, which is their name for white man. I contemplated a word I knew for black man. They're not the same thing.

He sat in the front passenger seat with his elbow out the open window. I sat directly behind him with my arm out the window. I decided to smack his elbow and tell him he hit a bird. I gave him a good scare, but he knew I didn't have feathers.

I sat there before the Eiffel Tower and looked up the vast reaches of steel before me. I imagined I would feel more complete by the time I made it to Paris, but life did not freeze in some climactic epiphany. Rather, I reminded myself that I am here. Now. And there is presently nowhere else I am, so I should enjoy it, because I will spend a lot of time in my life not being here.

The stewardess came back with the basket of spare bread. I took some and *merci'd* her. When she came back a third time, I asked if any bread was left. She said no, but the boy across the aisle didn't finish his. She asked if it was okay to touch it with her fingers and I told her I wouldn't have it any other way.

We sat outside the Parisian cafe munching on crepes and baguettes. I rolled up a piece of paper to look like a cigarette in the picture. The cafe owner took a picture of us, but it was overexposed and my paper didn't show up. Probably for the better, though, since one day, in-laws will see it.

She asked why I had taken so long in the outhouse. I told her I had to stop and do 100 pull-ups on my way back and it doesn't really take me that long to poo.

I had made a goal to kiss a local girl during the 8 hours I was in France. Now I know how it feels…to fail to achieve my goals.

She sent me a message saying hurry up and come home! I told her I'm trying, but that's the trouble with scheduled airline reservations.

Desperation
9/1/2012

Desperation.
Sit here—sit here for a while
soak in it.
Realize it.
Realize your desperation.
Take several minutes to let the thirst build.
This is worship—
the moment you realize your
desperation.

A deer only pants for water
when it is dying.

Could You Plant Yourself By Water?
9/13/2012

Could you plant yourself by water
and just stare out at the sea,
could you live life on your feet again
and see the world with me?

Your lips are on my mind again
like kisses in the hair
so pack your bags to leave and then
we'll head for anywhere.

Go sink your roots into the sand,
you'll go out with the tide.
Your hair will turn to seaweed and
you'll wash up by my side.

I'll pick you up out of the surf
and hold your salty hand.
forever you can be my mermaid;
I will be your man.

9/14/2012 ak

Softness-soaked slivers,
ribbons sifted through salt—
let loose your lavender lips
in palisades and parking lot.

They're softer and softer,
you age so well,
but you'd better not blame me,
The Old Kiss And Tell.

9/20/2012

I was looking up at that day's sky
when the summer turned to fall.
The dampened leaves at once grew cold
and I gave you a call.
The crisper air became our chests,
those melancholy lungs,
would fill with harvest festivals
and children having fun.
I picture you inside that house
at Colorado height,
and once more from Chicago yearn
for ancient summer nights.
Behind the wall of autumn lies
this memory of heat.
And looking back, that kiss becomes
again so bittersweet.

Warmer Nights
10/3/2012

I'm finding that I'm stuck in here
where time can always disappear
and days and nights don't go by fast or slow.
It seems the winter's closing in,
and soon it will be soft again,
and we will wear a lot of clothes.

    (Chorus)
    My clothes don't fit right, I can't sleep at night
    I need your summer eyes.
    My feet can't walk straight, I stay up too late
    in search of warmer nights
    (That I just haven't found quite yet)

I blink, another day flies by,
the sun can set before your eyes,
won't give you any warning till it's gone.
I've seen those grey clouds overhead,
and wondered who can live with it
when seas are waiting somewhere in the sun.

    (Chorus)

No beauty in fluorescent lights,
I need to run around outside
and jump into the ever-rolling waves,
but there's a lot here hindering
the little voice that's whispering
"My son, just place your hope in summer days."

    (Chorus)

An Ode to Kissing
October, 2012 ak

I kissed you on the cheek one time,
but that did not suffice.
So I kissed you on the lips one time,
then had to do it twice!
You said they'd be much better, were
we not in parking lots.
I guess the only way to know
Is kiss! And kiss a lot!

I know you have a quiet soul
that hides itself away.
I thought that I had found it once
on that December day.
But woe to me! Was I so wrong
to think I'd figured you!
So here I sit with open hands,
your heart now to pursue.

Hancock
10/27/2012
(Written on the 96th floor lounge of the Hancock tower at midnight)

She said, 'I'm just all about texture.'
We're reading minds dozens of metres above
the illuminated earth.
Thank you for carpet, engraved with the blood,
sweat, and tears of
the brains of hundreds of dead artists.
Why strive for the heavens, oh Babel?
Why not be content on the sand?
I rested there all summer as
my body healed itself.
Humans never found love in the heavens—
(until It came to us)
we found it in the rain.
I
look back at the day a forest misted around us.
We were dressed like Adam,
but the purity of the water distracted us.

Do you see us more clearly here, God,
when we ascend to metal heights?
Or do you prefer to come to us,
to bend low and pick us up?
I love You more because of this,
because You were restrained.
Not out of pride or arrogance,
the Maker was contained.

And
11/7/2012

And I'll start this with an And
because in life there is no pause.
You can't put it down and walk away,
or stop it with a clause.
I'd wake up so much earlier
and learn to read my dreams
if I could exegete your skin,
materialize your seams.
But life won't stop for these two birds,
we harbingers of life.
There's no conjunction to divide
a good friend from a wife.
So roll along through sentences—
across my roads and land,
I will continue to pursue
an endless beauty and...

Beautiful Felon
11/25/2012

You're a bird off a mountain that soars into flight;
you're the predator's howl in the dark of the night
that sends whispers of shivers my spine to my head
as you skip your first stone on a dry river bed.
My eyelids must like you—they draw you in sleep,
they've painted your mural, a Greek masterpiece,
from the wraps of my brain to the right cerebellum,
broke in and graffitied like a Beautiful Felon.

You're the thief of my thoughts—you're a real Robin Hood,
'cause you take what is bad and you make it all good.
You're a treacherous villain who's wanted for crimes,
such as stealing my heart and burning my time.
Soon you'll be an inmate at Heartbreaker's Jail;
they'll lock you up tight till you're ghostly and pale,
and I'll call it all just, 'cause you got what was coming,
but I can't hold you down so you're better off running.

I'll chase you down hard, Oh good felon of mine!
I'll put you in handcuffs and make you do time.
I don't trust the bars because you could slip through,
and I don't trust a guard 'cause he's easily fooled.
So I have no other choice but to hold you myself—
to wrap you up tight with a right and a left.
For all that you've done, and to stop further harm,
I'll hold you forever, in both of my arms.

Sky
11/26/2012 ak

Sail me out to sea, there's a star I gotta see,
gotta know if she's the diamond that was cut to fit in me.

Take me to the hills, cause there's a tree I gotta find,
gotta know if I can touch it, climb as high as I can climb.

(Bridge)
And you look at me, you've painted me a man I cannot be
so when you find out I'm a child, will you stay or will you flee,

> *(Chorus)*
> Oh, Sky, fly and set me free
> Sky, I'll hold you safely on the center of my wings
> Sky, just hold on tight to me
> Oh, sky, just ask me
> and I'll fly you to the lands you see in dreams
> (lands you've never seen)
> Oh, Sky

Wheel me to the west, cause there is gold yet to be found,
I need your effervescence as you dance and shine around
(Oh come on, leave the ground!)

And lead me to the east, so that we can find our home,
it's almost time for us to find a place to call our own.

(Bridge)
And I look at you, I paint a siren singing loud and true
and when I crash against the rocks, will I sink into the blue

> *(Chorus)*

(Misc.)
Where all the seashells cut our calloused feet,
we'd swim inside the summer's heat,
your voice can cut a blade of grass,
makes my heart slip off beat.
And there's a song that's stuck inside your head,
a tune that only I can sing
I think I sang it once to you,
but then you lost it in a dream.
Sometimes you dream of diners,
where we empty out our banks,
sometimes your dreams are empty rooms
with echoes in the blanks
I think I found you once,
your eyes saw deep inside my skin,
I taught you how to dance
and put one finger on your chin and said
Sky

(Chorus)

12/8/2012
A Rap

Boston to Tennessee, lager to Hennessy,
man, we grew up, Jonny Depp's Public Enemies.
Hop over to Denver, say what's up to Deborah,
we used to call this magic like 'abra cadabra,'
but now we write our own shows,
now we buy our own clothes,
now we hit a city till it's shaken like a snow globe
used to bump a Jetta, now I bum all rides,
summer on the beach got me tanner than a rawhide.

New York to Little rock, call my knuckles grid lock,
I don't kill Bloods, but I'll teach you how to Crip Walk.
Impact Nigeria, I'm the co-president,
used to hide Jesus, only now I'm less hesitant.
Over to Chicago, they tell me that the wind blows,
say when storms come, better roll up all the windows,
but this isn't my first winter, say hello to Ice Man.
Jesus makes it rain more than Condoleezza Rice can

Hats off to Bita, the Venezuelan chica,
took me to New York to hear Tim Keller the preacher.
That boy makes it rain, that boy is insane
that boy will preach the Bible till it's comin' out your brain

Globetrotting erryday like you caught me out of Harlem,
for lack of definition, dear, I'd love to call you darlin'.
Feisty little appetites that paint me like a scene,
now come on home, my white canary, tell me where you've been.
I'm hungry for the heart in you, the thinking that you do,
I'd love to make myself a hat and rest on top of you.
With every single drop of me that knows you with my eyes,
I'd love to take you far away and waste away our lives.

12/15/2012, but technically 2:12am on the 16th   ak

   I sat next to you and
we watched time pass by slowly.
We saw the alley rats play tag, and
I heard the gaps grow into hours as
our conversation ended and you slept.
Your sleep is only the result of your
brain painting brightly colored
thoughts on daylight.
It may rearrange some things
and not quite get all the facts right,
but it'll do the job.

   I see you dancing now.
You and your friends in a bar
I never knew the name of.
Come dance with me.
Come sleep on my couch
and I will sleep on the floor beside you.

   I see that night we spent in Indiana,
where your dreams woke me in
the middle of the night,
I thought they were beautiful.
Breakfast took you back in time;
I saw your face without years.

   I hear you saying honest things now.
My patience exhausts itself on telephones
and handwritten letters. May they never suffice.
They are no airplane.
They will not connect my fingers to
your fingers,
or my lips to your hair,
and you are not a photograph.

Call Me Bumble Bee
12/1/2012, 1:30am

And what about we, the wandering class?

I look at men like Shane Claiborne and others I know personally who are in love with homeless people. I admire them so much. It may even be an envy. I need to care more.

Then there are those called to a stable congregation, like my roommate Aaron: Live here, minister here and die here. Disciple these people and give your life to them. I should heed Ewan McGregor's advice from *Beginners*: "We experienced a certain sadness our parents never had time for." Today, I accomplished very little, which is probably why I feel so restless now at 1:30am.

However, I can never help but wonder about us. What about we, the wandering class? I'm too restless to be a pastor but too timid to be a full-time missionary. God, don't settle me down quite yet. Please.

We wanderers have yet a spark of lust in our eye. We can't build a home, but we can sure pass through one like a ghost…though it seems that even ghosts are more settled than I. They can haunt the same home for centuries. I shiver.

No, my ministry is not in the urban streets of America's style factories, nor is it permanently the rolling hills of her spine. She has treated me well on my sojourn here, my launching stone to the globe. If only this garden came with a map. Yet here I am, following my nose to whichever bushel of flowers smells sweetest. Oh, how these scents change with the wind! Name me bumble bee.

And what about we, the wandering class,
which is too thick to move, yet too fine to grasp?
See, I had this idea that I'd take you with me,
and for better or worse, we'd run for the sea.
Upon reaching shore we would hire a boat,
and sail east, west or elsewhere, or merely go float.
And arriving away at new tropical coasts,
we would wander around, just some new-to-town ghosts.
Sometimes we would run, sometimes I'd carry you,
and we'd grow old together—two colors, one hue.
Like a delicate drink is fermented with time,
we'd blend till our flavors made Pinot Noir wine.
My body of violet, and yours of clear white,
We'd sleep at the sunrise and run through the night.
In motion and sound would our legacy be,
vibrations colliding and smoothing the seams.

One stitch equals two, as one kiss demands more,
but a tear in our fabric subtracts at least four.
So sew us together with spider-like webs,
but make room for our foot soles and holes for our heads.
We'll breathe and run faster than ever before,
just you and me running—let's go find a shore.

12/6/2012

Like filler words coming from a filler man's mouth,
I close my eyes gently, and hear you go south.

Some late night thoughts that I have found here, heavy in my head,
don't know if I can hold them, they're too heavy for my pen.
You've got your fingers wrapped around a heart that's been made clean,
a garden of desires you want no one else to see.
With daffodils and sleeping pills, your garden came to bloom
in perfect timing, not your own, not later or too soon.
I wandered through it once or twice, this garden of your thoughts,
got turned around and finally found that I was surely lost.
No time to stop and calculate, no time to catch my breath—
just time to walk away from you and speak some words of death.
Your flowers quickly wilted then, admitting their defeat.
In blinded youth, I lost all couth, and crushed them with my feet.
I see that I'm a culprit here, for your withholding ways.
I broke new soil, learned some things, and traded death for praise.
I know I can't apologize for my sophomoric words,
but if I could, I'd trade them all for kisses on your hurts.
And after I'd made clear to you my sorrowful regret,
I'd try to love you, hard as flame, with gentleness instead.

So open up your ancient doors, swing open ancient gates!
We no longer have use for you, you cutting words of hate!
Just let me plant this single seed, which one day will become
a dowry of long almond branches blooming in the sun!
A symbol of my love, my love—the one that takes its time
to test its soil, deepen roots, and stretch out like a vine.
I'll do my best to wait for you, oh little almond tree,
and when you bloom, I will rejoice, and carry you with me.

12/17/2012

And we laid down an army of ten thousand strong,
an army of artists that fought with their song.
We lay them down gently, they went without fight,
the way every good day will still end in night.

Their army drew arms, but we drew ours first,
they fought us with slingshots and shouted and cursed.
We unholstered handguns, our tanks and grenades;
we even shot missiles upon their parades.

This army of artists, so peaceful and pure,
were not spared the onslaught they had to endure.
Their bodies went flying and scattered around;
our weapons got larger, made uglier sounds.

We had them cut off; they had no where to go,
till one tiny artist stood up and said no.
He closed both his eyes, cleared his cute little throat
and launched into song using mysterious notes.

His voice carried shivers down all of our spines
and sent vibrato quivers up all our TEC-9's.
His song made trees dance, and it healed up the earth
till somebody shot him and he fell in the dirt.

12/27/2012, 5:43am

There's a hand touching fingers
touching knuckles touching fingers and
a swarm of blankets around us.
Your feet wrapped up in my arms.

I'd keep this moment.

I'd name it and never let it out to play.
I'd frame it and put plastic magnets
against it on the fridge—
for guests to see.
Then our lips touched,
soft plungers in good hands.

2013

THE YEAR I STARTED GROWING OUT MY HAIR

My years at Moody were not bad by any means, but they certainly do not fill exciting pages of memoirs the way other years of my life do.

I began the year dating an old friend of mine, but it lasted about two months before we realized that we should have just remained friends, not lovers. My first year at Moody was tumultuous, as I mentioned last year, as I adjusted from several years of rootless travel, but it was good. It was humbling. By the end of my first year, I had made some good friends and even started some traditions and a new ministry on the campus, which is still running at the time of this writing.

As I slid into the summer, I seemed to be entering a new season of maturity and solidity in who I was. I began reading Christian mystic writers and spending time in contemplative prayer.

I returned to Colorado and, as memory serves (though it's probably more fantastic in my memory than it was in reality), I seemed to be with friends up in the mountains adventuring and camping every other day.

If I were to write a history of my dating life, it would be called 'Bad Timing: The Life and Dates of Ethan Renoe.' I started seeing a girl at the tail end of summer, before flying back to Cape Cod for a visit, then on to Chicago, and the timing was so poor we didn't really get the chance to know each other well enough to pursue a real relationship.

Back at Moody, my familiarity with the campus grew and I became more and more implanted into the community. The year ended with a spontaneous road trip to Kansas City to attend the OneThing conference...

1/13/2013 ak

My memory flies coach as my lips
sail farther and farther away from yours
through the friendly blue skies
once more toward Chicago.
The eyes in my face sag,
longing—of their own volition—
to sleep and dream of you.
They dream the way sand dreams;
that brackish water will cover them
and take them through the sea to
brighter coasts.
I touched your hand and yours
met mine, but the skin is irrelevant.
We touched each other mutually;
more than bodies connected.

I think I hear you say to me:
> break and break again.

Everything has already crumbled;
our armageddon rolled in like thunder.
It fell quiet as a heap of snow
and rose up like a lion from sleep.
Kiss me.
Quickly.
I think this may be my purpose in life:
to kiss those lips the Lord put right there,
below your nose.

And oh, how I would hold you there;
non-keratinized stratified squamous
to epithelium.
Tissue to tissue.
Lip to lip.
We could lay down in the winter and let it
freeze us there together,
lips touching, fingers in hair.
We'd never forget and we'd never
grow old.

Now I think I say to you:
> break and break again.

I know my claws already sank deep into your hide,
letting blood like lotion from a nozzle.
I saw a death underwater.
She didn't make a sound, but her blood lifted from her.
Her body slowly sank.
Give me your heart
and I will let you bleed into me,
the ocean that surrounds you.

Why Summer Is Better Than Every Other Season
2/3/2013

Do you spend your life dying or spend it alive?
I looked for a winner but none had survived.
What is love but a weight on the neck of a friend,
a satirical compound that explodes in the end.
Have you found this joy yet, or are boots on your feet?
I think you're looking for something bred in the heat.
This beast was Behemoth, it never was tamed.
They fed it the ocean and gave it a name.
Its name wasn't winter or springtime or fall,
they named her the summer; she's fairer than all.
I tasted her lips in the mist of the woods.
She touched me with raindrops, washed me where I stood.
But this joy ran away to a hot humid day,
and despite how we beckon, it's there she will stay.

A Note from Starbucks
2/10/2013

He squeezed himself between two seats in the coffee shop. He smelled like old coffee and house taxes, and had a briefcase overflowing with papers to prove it. Poor guy. Some people are meant to be boring, but without them, the world would fall apart. Who would audit us? Who would transfer our funds to the president's accounts? Boring people are the glue of the world. People who use words like 'equity,' 'financing,' and 'downpayment' spin this world around.

2/12/2013
All these snippets were on the same page of a notebook. You can see how they morphed into the song 'The Center of the Storm' on the following page.

We've been tearing up our feet on these foreign lands,
breaking down train tracks with these shackles on our hands.
But where have we been that our voice has been known?
I've spent 22 years in search of a home.
Your lips gently healed me, and broke off a chain.
They gave me this freedom not found without pain.

———————————

Don't be broken, I can break you myself.
These hands haven't killed, but this mouth can raise hell.
I saw you once on New Year's, when our voices were
        (Unfinished)

———————————

I held a golden hand with the skin on my teeth,
and it bit me on the lip.
I held you once on New Year's Eve
and your voice gave me a tip,
you said everyone dies, so you better live now.
We're dancing at the speed of sound.
We're falling off the Eiffel Tower,
wake me up before we hit the ground.
Your eyes once lit me up
with radiance within.
It wasn't till I let you go
did clarity begin.

———————————

We sat in coffee shops like church
and had a thing for late night diners.
I kissed you once on New Year's Eve
and then your eyes retired.

This freedom that you gave to me
arrived on your departure.
I flew with arrow's liberty,
your airplane was the archer.
I broke all your piano strings
and threw away the keys.
I kissed you on the balcony
and weakened both your knees.
But like a paper aeroplane,
I had to let you go.
I folded up your softer spots
and gave a little throw.
I used to try to tell myself,
we're old until we're not.
This birth and birth and rebirth
only dies if you get caught,
so I led you to the train tracks,
and I bound you with my rope.
I laid you down so gently
that you thought there may be hope.
With teary eyes and last goodbyes,
we waited for a train,
and when it came, I looked away,
and waited for the pain.
With this farewell, our memories
were scattered on the tracks,
like how we used to wander
with the sunrise at our backs,
or all those late night coffee runs,
or all the broken doors.
In terms of our adventure, darling,
we were never poor.
I see that day we saw the sky
grow bluer than your eyes.
I sang to you in thunderstorms
but rain can't harmonize.

The Center of the Storm
February, 2013

Looking back, I think I spent
a good part of my life
preparing for and thinking about
the day I'd say goodbye (to you).
I see all our midnight coffee runs
and all those broken doors.
In terms of our adventures darling,
we were never poor.

> *(Chorus)*
> Now you're the center of the storm, oh,
> but help is on the way.
> Let's say goodbye tomorrow
> because I need another day.
> Without you, I'm an empty room,
> just throw away the keys,
> but with you we're both trapped in here,
> so go on now, be free.

We spilled ourselves across the states,
the sunrise on our backs
and I think of how I kissed you
on Chicago's railroad tracks.
We fled to Philadelphia
where you apologized.
I saw your eyes glow gray
beneath that corridor of skies.

> *(Chorus)*

I spoke to you in thunderstorms
and filled my quill with drips,
then fashioned you a letter
in an old forgotten script.
And I sent it to you on the wind,
I watched it sail away
and I prayed to God for silence
because there's nothing left to say.

(Chorus)

Skin is the Problem
2/13/2013

skin is the problem.
It's that embrace when your fingers
graze her gentle skin through her
open-backed dress.

skin is the problem.
It's when, in an old photograph,
the dimples in her cheeks take you back
to that night spent on her couch,
exploring the caverns of each others' mouth.

skin is the problem.
It's the reason you can't get over her,
it's the reason you want her back.
It's the cause of all your sorrow,
and the penny on the track.

skin is the problem,
When you swim in the sea,
it's the weightless fingers holding you
beneath the surface of the blue glass.

It's skin.

It's all skin.

I asked you to wash me, to take all my scars,
so you kissed me so gently in the back of a car.
Your quiet lips sang with the touch of a cheek
in the language of lovers forbidden to speak.
The hospital watched us in silence and woe,
as I held you so closely, resigned to let go.
And let go I did, and now let go I have,
as this ramshackled gangster's relearning his craft.

2/19/2013 ak

I think I'm close to letting go,
to saying my goodbyes,
I think your turn to let it show
is slowly on the rise.
I long to pull it out of you,
like spring's extracted teeth,
but wait I have and wait I will,
your feelings to unsheath.
I found this place inside of me
that I have tried to heal,
the goal is pain, not scarlessness,
but I still can't seem to feel.
I think I'm close to moving on,
to thinking of you less.
I see that night you slept on me,
your head upon my chest.
I hear your quiet whimpering,
feel twitches in your sleep.
I know he hurt that place in you,
but that pain's not yours to keep.
If I could only heal you now,
I'd kiss you with my mouth.
I'd kiss away those things he did
that bind you to the south.
But you're so far away from me,
in sleep your eyes are closed,
so sleeplessly I'll think of you
and try to produce prose.
Your quiet lips did love me well,
I haven't one regret.
I tried to kiss away your fear,
but both our cheeks got wet.
I'd hold you now if you were here,
like oceans hold the land.
Like two old friends in winter walk,

I'd take you by the hand.
We'd see the places that I kept,
and maybe see yours too,
as friends with years beneath our belts,
I'd say goodbye to you.
I think I'm close to letting go,
to closing both my eyes.
I'll leave your heartfelt winter kiss
in search of warmer skies.

2/25/2013

I'm looking for we who read the world in the same way. It's a search bred more out of a desire for art than community. Depiction is essential. Perception is crucial. Can we use old film in slow motion to capture those scenes of our youth? We're running through forests with girls on our backs. We got lost on an island and couldn't find the ocean. They may call it Babylon, but I prefer Home. A beauty perceived with eyelids closed is no beauty at all.

How much more has life taught me than my child in the womb of my unmarried wife? I haven't known her yet—in any sense—but right now, I think about ice cream. I think about teaching my child the art of licking it so no drips run down over their fingers.

(It looks like the pen went dry)

3/8/2013 4:30am
On the Orange Line to Midway Airport

More awake than anyone when it's four
in the morning and all I had was naps in my pocket.
The world takes a while to wake up
and I moved faster than
anything else in Chicago.
I heard the bums talk about respect as I
waited for the shuttle. I ate my bagel.
I waded away from our young conversation
in the coffee shop three hours prior,
and out into the blackness of morning;
the tip of your nose and the youth
of your eyelashes becoming more
and more
distorted by the ripples.
Black lady on the train teaches me how to fly
like the pigeon on the tracks.
I looked at it after flight in the
early morning dark.
Her heavy wings dragged on the ground
like she carried groceries.
Speak to me, I told it.
Preach to me, I told it.
And in the blackness of the morning,
I learned to leave the ground.

Easter Night
3/31/2013

This toast,
to the night in the church, dancing till our limbs,
dripping with sweat,
became heavy as hammers
and closed forever the lid
to the grave of our Lord.
May it ever be vacant.
May we ever dance when we remember,
may we ever rejoice at His name.

A girl in grayscale polka dots,
a girl dressed all in red,
a girl too short to ask to dance,
a girl that spun my head.
She wore her golden camisole,
I wore a holey tee.
I almost got the guts to ask
that girl to dance with me.
She spun away, beyond the grip
of subtle verbal queries,
and into that oblivion, where
the sound is never carried.
I danced tonight, Chicagoland,
I danced all over you.
I worshipped resurrected Kings,
the One, in fact (not two).
My heavy arms were burning
and my legs forgot to breathe.
My head was foggy as the church
like fuzzy TV screens.

I missed that night before it ended,
it slipped too far away.
depressingly, this night again
will fade on into day.
I hate the way that time moves on,
though moments be not sweet.
If every one could last a year:
a week per pulsing beat.
Tonight I opened both my eyes
to find that I could see
the many people, lonely souls,
all suffering with me.

It led me to a church dance in Chicago.
I thought about what a strange
bar had hidden itself
within
and next to
the church dance floor,
but there it was,
fueling our jive.
Commanding our movement.
Directing our fun.
Whether or not we control ourselves, I do not know.
But I do know a gift when I see one,
and tonight, Christmas morning,
disguised as Easter,
had left tonight
beneath the tree.

Unsent Letter
Spring, 2013

Dear Lemon,

My flight was delayed from 4:20 to 8:20, so here I sit in the recent darkness, waiting for my plane to arrive and take me back to Chicago. As you know, I really don't like Chi-town at all, and the subtraction of your constant communication from my life didn't make things any easier. Let me say this up front: I'm not writing this as an attempt to win you back or anything like that. I simply want to finalize the closure of our 'romantic' relationship/return to friendship, and get a few things off my chest.

First, I had a blast dating you. You are one of the most fun people I've ever met, and we simply got along flyingly. I think we made the right decision looking back, though, for a number of reasons.

...

I miss you a lot and it's no easier when I see pictures from the fashion show, or you just hanging with your friends having fun. <u>I am really so glad that you're loving your life and your roomies! I'm really stoked for you and hope your joy only increases!</u>

I, on the other hand, have not had the greatest semester ever. It's been pretty rough, actually. I trust that God will bring me out of it and bring redemption and fruit from this season, but it just has not come yet. I think I had my hopes set so high for you to be 'the one,' but it just seems that God had other plans. He definitely showed me a lot about my own heart, and how I put so many things and people above Him in my life. I feel like I idolized you in that sense, and that quickly led to my not being the spiritual leader I should have been, both to you and to everyone else; not to mention the immense amount of pressure that would have put on you.

I can't remember exactly why I started this letter, or what, exactly I wanted you to take away from it. I know that more than anything, I hope that we can be good friends as we were before. I know that takes time, and it's not just a switch we can hit to return to normal. I hope that you still feel free to talk to me anytime about anything!

Well, Killer, I'm gonna wrap it up here. I really hope you're doing awesome and you take whatever time you need to move on, but I definitely hope you do and we can go on many more adventures together! I know you said you hope we can still write letters, so here it is! Letter numero uno as friends again! Talk to you soon Killer,

Your friend,

Ethan

P.S.— Sorry this has been so tough for me. I know you said it has been easier for you, which I am really happy for, but as you know, it's been tough for me.
P.P.S.— I still don't think I ever told you the P.P.S. story!

Underbelly
4/13/2013

I was the collective youth in search of the other side of America.
I sure tried my hardest
to turn it over like a child turns a fat lady over on the beach,
just to find his body blanketed in more sand than results.
And lay there, America did.
I tried to dive into it.
I sought out the deepest parts of the continent,
but left with nothing but a
ticket in my pocket reporting my feeble attempts.
I left that beach with nothing but glass in my knuckles
and a silent alarm ringing in my ears.

I was the collective youth that knew their longings
would be satisfied upon their immersion
into the cavernous underbelly of an idealized dream.
That underbelly did come at a cost, though.
A high price was paid to realize that that dream we all shared
is as solid as the evaporation of water.

So I got wet.

I grew up and found joy in the ocean.
Mobilized by salt, my Bible got sand in its binding,
but my skin was happy.

The Spirit is the Story
4/20/2013

An impassioned night.
The night I found out Laura broke up with Nick,
making her a single mother.
I listened to her weep on the phone,
prayed,
and watched *Submarine.*
I don't know why I become this passionate,
but I am glad for it.
Aaron sleeps silently in the bed behind me.
Once in a while, he shifts,
and occasionally moans.
I sit here, never wanting to sleep again,
but to drive until August forces me back to my studies,
to pray into a timeless eternity,
to run on a beach that never leads to a factory.

And once we hear the sirens singing us to sleep,
I know the fear within my mind
is surrendered to that of my dreams.
I know you'll turn around and be the face I've grown old with.
I know You're everywhere.
There's a wading into moving water that astounds those
who have never been taken out by it.
I forgot a bright-eyed summer,
and the freedom that it brought me,
rich with granola and toothpaste.
When I flew to Africa,
(my wings got tired)
my toothpaste spilled into my backpack.
I think I've lost hold of the stories I used to tell.
I think they're less of my life
and more of a reel of 8mm film I play before spectators.
I think I'll go get lost.

Does the Lord command an audience,
or have we just traded in
a heart we held with infant hands
for robots that we've trained within?
I once was lost inside a church,
the lights were all turnt out.
I screamed at bloody murderers
and all the girls would shout.
How long ago did I grow up,
this vomit on my skin?
I swear I didn't mean to,
I looked away as he crept in.

Cape Cod, I'm chasing a youth I left somewhere on this peninsula.
I may have left it beneath a giant red X,
or in the attic of a church,
or in a surf shop.
I'm looking for a living, breathing story.
Holy Spirit, are you this story that's deeper than words?
I tell it so You can breathe life into it.
You're the magic in the words,
You're the timelessness of nostalgia.

I love You,

I love You,

I love You.

We got lost on the way to the map store.
There is no padded dirt on the way to the Lord.
On His mountain, there is no air-conditioned picnic table;
there's a passion you can't touch,
but you can bushwhack your way to His toes.

Now, where were we going?
Were we driving toward the sunrise,
or away from it?
I'm out of danger, but not out of longing—
a pining for your touch,
for your shoulder under my fingertips.
I see you naked in the snow that day,
and I see the scars hidden beneath your skin.

Don't hide from them by removing your clothes.

I can see in your eyes hints of a fear you never named,
of a brother you never embraced.
But hear me now, hear this:
Your tracks have derailed my train,
if only your lips knew my name.

5/22/2013

Break you?
See, I'll tell the broken that they're sewn together.
I will tell the beauty that she deserves not to have cuts on her arms
and bruises on her face.
bring justice, oh Lord,
and hurry. The wicked are many.

But, break you?
Splinter your shoulders and wrench your back?
I'll hold you tighter than that.
My fingers and your skin connect on a level
no movie can capture in film.
Perhaps intimacy is cleaner on a screen,
from a third party spying,
but a risk I can take
is that I'm the one who will break.

Break me, break me,
I find myself humbled.
don't forsake me,
my words were just jumbled.
I forgot that we die,
but we don't die alone.
Some people hold hands
and others go home.
But I held you too long
and our words were too few.
I watched you fall down
when I let go of you.
On sidewalks you broke
and my tears made you clean,
the winter was long,
but your grave is now green.

And my friend wrote a song
about how he is sick,
and he died on the weekend
as thin as a stick.
I long for an answer,
to know where he went:
to see angels or demons,
or live in a tent?
If there is no middle
and we must pick a side,
then how do we get there,
and where is the line?
I've loved for much less
than a kiss on the cheek,
on that night in the hospital
or that wintery week.

The point is, I'm searching
for what's in between
this lonely death dying
and living the dream.
If God is so present,
so faithful and near,
then why don't I feel Him,
His words in my ear?
I long to be held
as I hold onto her,
my beautiful wife
with no clothes to deter.
Some day we will get there,
one day we'll arrive,
but I continue searching
and try to survive.

To My Wife
7/16/2013

Can we travel?
Then we'll sleep for a while,
letting roots grow where they will.
And then, can we travel?
Returning once again,
holding hands in our grass.
I'll look at your eyes as
you peer into me, but
the moment will be cut short as we leave
once again
to travel.

7/30/2013 aw

Like a cryptic triptych, it's hard to describe
why Jesus would save me and show me the light.
Like a mystic diptych, I've folded away
these battalions of thought that try to keep you at bay.

Like a cryptic triptych, you're hard to describe.
You're hard to hold onto and hard to deny—
I set you down hard like a case full of Jack
but you woke me again when you quickly came back.
I saw through your eyes, but I guarded my own,
I picked up some eggshells and called them my home.

And what I need is collision.
What I need is for my fingers to dig trenches
in your palms,
for our heads to fuse at the mouth.
I'll let my arms be rusted trunks
above the superficial roots which sink
down
        down
                down into your arms.
We are one. We have won.
In multiplicity, we admit defeat
as they bury us in the soil.
Together:
Two old trees with twisted branches.

Awaken me, O weary dream,
and end this conscious suffering.
For I do not want you to see
this rage that lives inside of me.
This fire ever haunts my bones,
and tears down nations all alone.
The Philistines and Babylon
have held us here for far too long.
So blow and billow, arch your back,
the ghosts no longer will attack.

Oh Sister, Sister, let me in,
we never saw what could have been.
With eyes for lips, your heart should know
that where you're looking, kisses blow.
My arms were weak before with you;
my strength had lifted like the dew.
Oh, weary dream, return once more
and rest this tired ship ashore.
Return to me those sunset eyes,
and in their passion, be baptized.

Unsent Letter
8/13/2013 aw

Dear W,

I'm sitting at the gate of the airport as the night slowly eases its grip on the light, letting the first rays of the dawn slip through the window behind me. As I said before, my tendencies in an airplane, airport and other air-related things, are to wax nostalgic and poetic. I've spent a long time looking for a thing I couldn't see, but when I finally could touch it I found it lived in me. I've always enjoyed wrapping my fingers around things I could wrap my fingers around, which is why it took me so long to embrace the concept of God. The concept of something bigger than me loving me. Crazy.

Now I'm on board the aircraft, sandwiched between two not-so-fun-sized gentlemen. It's kind of cozy in a way. Like two big skin-covered teddy bears. As I write, my eyes grow heavy with the weight of an early, early morning. I won't last too long.

So as I wait for takeoff, when I can finally allow my mind to once more be at rest, I find my brain seeking out innocent curiosities. Curiosities such as—why would a beautiful, wild-haired girl (with such great skin) such as yourself be attracted to a mustachioed goon like me? I guess we'll never know. Despite such curiosities, I don't want either of us to breed and harness unwarranted hopes, leading to unnecessary heartache and pain. I hope you guard your heart as I attempt to guard mine, yet the angel of heartbreak warfare is rarely fair in her dealings. So, as stated that night as we lay on our backs with our feet in the swings, stars racing overhead, let's just keep talking. Let's just keep lettering. Nothing more.

Now I'm on my second flight, this one from Nashville to Boston. I'm sitting by a scientist who can do quantum physics on his fingers, but misses belt loops when he gets dressed in the morning. I re-read what I wrote earlier, and despite my pseudo-intellectualism, I really just spat out a bunch of nonsense. Apologies.

I just read the first five chapters of the Gospel of Luke and noticed something. I noticed how many people it says are filled with the Holy Spirit—even before Jesus is born! Like Anna, who was married for seven years, then widowed until she was 84. It says that she was in the temple all day, every day, worshipping, praying and fasting! That's mind-blowing to me. Despite the fact that she could have simply remarried, since she was probably still pretty young, she chose to be in the temple with God instead! What does that say to the differences in satisfaction of marriage vs. worship? I want to get to that place.

> I'm up here in the plane today,
> you're down there skipping stones.
> I'm worth my weight in gold, they say;
> you're worth your weight in bones.
> This cocktail napkin epitaph
> assumes that love is real.
> So let's trade in our worshipping
> for something we can feel.

And now, we have achieved mundanity! These letters are now routine. The first few are of utmost import, but now that we are colloquially 'pen pals,' we must stretch and reach for subjects to write on. We exchange poems, thoughts, observations from our lives. Now that we have less time to spend together, these letters become more meaningful, more fresh. And that's a good thing! Letters delivered by hand during time spent together are one thing, but letters in the mail during times of long absence become so much sweeter. I'm landing in Boston now. Stay tuned for Cape Cod pictures!

(Unfinished)

Undated recorded moment with Bita
Summer, 2013

"Can you promise me something, Ethan?" she asked as we sat hanging out the windows of her parked car, staring at the star-spangled sky.

"Sure," I said.

"Promise that we'll never stop going on adventures."

I laughed. Then I promised. It was almost the end of the summer. That melancholy last week before class resumes and schoolwork takes the place of summer breezes on our hands.

8/17/13 aw

I've got a letter in my notebook that I'm never gonna send
because you're mad at me and honestly, it's never gonna end.
I tried to kiss you quietly, to ease your numbing pain,
but oh, so great is your mistake, it soaked you like the rain.

Now the hammers ever beat my head and weight is piled on,
but twice He told me you were dead, so twice we saw the dawn.
Sing, Wake, O sleeper, see the light, look long and hard and true,
'cause what's in me is half as bright as what I see in you.

I traveled all around the world, but never could I see
'cause what I was forgetting, most importantly, was me.
I found that Thailand was a party; a poem was Brazil.
But native to my skin, I found a pride I couldn't kill.

So now I'm here out by the sea, I'm trapped inside a home.
'Cause what good is a summer house you're sitting in alone?
But praise the Mount, my God and King, His presence satisfies.
And may He grant me, evermore, to look into your eyes.

The light stabs my eyes like
the sunrise—my head by the window
on a pillow facing south.
I creep my eyes open to the flight stewardess
taking my trash.

If only she could take my trash.

If only she could wash me, make me clean.
My heart aches, it's empty as an earthquake.
Something shifts beneath my surface and I miss you.
Cracks arise from my ruptured crust
and thoughts about her nose
and her lips
tumble in. They have managed to drift,
devoid of gravity, to my core.

I kissed her at 2am one time.
We sat by a pool with our feet in the water.
August was gentler then,
and I didn't know her.

But now we wait for this plane
to take me elsewhere, to be the Spirit
that blows me where I submit.

I wrestled an angel once, over Facebook.
She turned out to be a vase full of milk
which I accidentally tapped with my archaeological hammer,
and the whole thing fell apart.

I never believed in skin until she touched me,
until her microscopic fingers touched my spine,
made the hairs on my bones stand up.
And I never trusted exit signs
until she left. It wasn't a decoration after all.
So I found out that some doors close.
I found that certain windows break,
and you cut your hand on the glass going in.

I've named this woman gravity—
I'm an airplane.
She is still in effect, but I found a way to fly.
Or maybe it's the other way around.
She ran so fast she broke free of the
barrier that nailed her to the ground.
Shot straight up into the air.
Crashed.

I'm still on an airplane now,
fearing the same thing she did.
I mean, if planes buried everyone they killed
instead of their survivors,
maybe more people would fly.
I have a survivor or two I'd like to bury myself.
I just keep telling myself, TIME KILLS ALL THINGS.
For today, I guess I'll kill more of my flesh.
I love watching it die.
It's time for new earthquakes to sound,
breaking ground and
letting in forgiveness.

The sidewalk is cool beneath the seats
of our pants.
Richard, the homeless man, and I
are watching a bike messenger smoke a cigarette.
Richard smokes one too
as I sit beside him.
I can't understand a darn word he says.

We are rock n' roll.

We got a turkey sandwich for Richard,
and some chips.
He told us it wasn't enough,
that we had to take him to the hospital
and pay for him too.
So we walked away.

We took our new Columbian swimsuit model
friend to a diner. Ate French toast
and she ate yogurt.
We told her we believed in God.
She told us she believed in energy.
Then we saw her after she went to the bathroom,
emerging with six inch heels and a dress
from France or Spain or something.
Told her she looked great.
And dropped her off at a bar.
It was three in the morning.

We had found her under fireworks,
as we watched from the pier.
She laughed a lot and
touched my arm, as
South Americans are wont to do.
She introduced us to her cousin and her friends,
who played in a metal band,
'chaos,' they called it.
Loved them all.

Then, Colombian in tow, we went
looking for an experience
and found a poem.

The Nomad's Anthem
Fall, 2013
Within the first couple of weeks at college, when I was deeply feeling the urge to move on once more, I penned this song in the back of my notebook during a ministry class.
Capo 3
C Am G F

Oh I've got that bug, I got that wandering bug again
It's itching at my foot soles and its gnawing on my head
I've got to fly, I've got to dip, I've think I've got somewhere to be
But girl you know your pretty lips already did so much for me
But there's a soul inside my skin he thinks he's Christopher Columbus,
Gotta sail, he's gotta run before he's just college alumnus
Girl you know I can't sit still, I'm restless like the waves.
They roll and move and tend to lose more ground now every day

    (Chorus)
    I know I'll find it, I'll find it someday
    By plane, car, greyhound, or the New York subway
    And when I get there, I'll take my boots off,
    I'll last a few days, Then probably move on

I got a call the other day, the road's lonely once more.
He said that he remembers me like ships remember shores.
I sat down here and planted roots, it was an accident I swear.
Because no matter where I am, I long for over there.

    (Chorus)

This city's walls have dried me out like a starfish on the rock
And though the lake is near, the coast is much too far to walk.
The ocean is my home, it is my permanent address.
'Cause if home is where the heart is, there's salt water in my chest.

    (Chorus)

Trains travel slowly.

Deserts without end. Memories fading in and out like balloons released by a limp-wristed four year old. Where is she? That girl I hid under the pool table with. It's more than a mountain vacation in the summer. It's a new home. I know you've been looking for one for quite some time now. Now you can be here. Now you can be safe where the mountains and trees surround you. Where the cities have no say in how you dress and who you are. Forget the passions you consumed with such fiery eagerness for the toned and fit bodies of the passing girls. They have fallen apart now. They followed after their souls. You, however, have stayed. You have done well to bury your talent in the ground and wait for a garden to grow. It has come indeed. It has sprung up from this fertile soil where you planted your experience, your time and your love. Caring, you walked into the kitchen with a hot apple pie in your mitts. With girth and circumference, you fed me that oven lovin'. I thanked you because you did feed me as I was, not as you wished I was.

We're still in that mountain home. It's more than a home, but you get the idea. It's an idyll. When I call it to memory, time still stands still. We can be in the sun. We can be indoors and enjoy hearing rain. Things still move slowly. The train has moved a mere meter. Why is it that heat is life? Photosynthesis. Things don't make sense unless you plant them once more in that fertile soil, resting in who you are. The seed doesn't make the seed grow, God does. I tried a few times and failed. I used to taste real bad.

Well, at any rate, we are leaving that home in the mountains now. We are heading for that summer house on the Cape. The one I've dreamed of since youth. Since I was lost in it as a college boy and wondered at the silent strength trapped within the old wood. It is a marvel. You could count the boards that make it if you wanted to. It smells like wet wood in the summer. It smells warm in the winter. I have eaten a good many meals there, and paced out the pages of my poems and works within the confines of her walls. Join me there. Let's tour. I'll teach you how to live on the Cape if you teach me how to be alive again.

11/24/2013

Thank God for permanent tan lines,
for sun and the beach and the sea.
Praise God for every last promise,
that He's faithful to you and to me.

I once found myself in an orchard,
but no fruit could be found on the trees.
No leaves and no greens,
no half-sprouted beans,
just a small rubber mallet for knees.

I looked all around for a face I could see,
but no visage was there to be found.
So I climbed all the branches
to see the expanses
of land, but lost sight of the ground.

I tried to climb down from that treetop,
but no gravity seemed to exist.
Now up was not up,
but down may have been up,
and a limb gave me cuts on the wrist.

I tell you this tale as a warning
about going alone through a forest.
you may think it's okay
to just wander away,
but a fool is the one who ignores it.

Sweet Dragonfly
12/25/2013 aa
Capo 3

C   G
And I fold like a broken flower in your pocket,
C   D   G
like a truth that you bear but you wish you forgot it.
C   G
We've got stories, we've got five years of memories,
C   D   C
and in five more, I doubt that you'll remember me.
Like the stories that you heard when you were a little girl
about a pirate and a princess who sailed around the world,
or a garden that you planted by your childhood home
all these thoughts of me will be gone, gone, gone

   (Chorus)
   G   C   G
   Sayin', my, oh my, oh my sweet dragonfly,
   G   D   G
   will you come back home and teach me how to fly?
   G   C   G
   Man oh man, if you ever get the chance
   G   Em   D   G
   come back to Chicago and teach me how to dance

Now I march and I hike till my legs go numb,
my feet get blisters and I bust a lung.
I'm looking for a beach I can call my home,
because I'm tired of walking this path alone.
So for now I'll just walk till my hair turns gray,
till my knees hit the dirt and I fade away.
The fire in my chest needs a fuel like You,
won't you pump the forge and walk with me too? (Woo!)

   (Chorus)

12/9/2013

I've been doing my living underground
and I've been haunting your letters like a ghost
and I've been doing my thinking in the clouds
among the moon and starry host.
In spite of me You meet me here,
I feel You moving in the earth.
You come and make me disappear;
You're giving me a second birth.

2014

FEELING DOWN IN CHICAGO

2014 started in Kansas City. Technically, in a shady bar in Kansas City. I walked out of the OneThing New Year's Eve celebration because there was too much peppy emotion and I wandered throughout the city to a dark bar. I walked to the corner, sat down, and started writing in a tiny pocket notebook.

That environment seemed far more 'real' to me than the strobe-light-and-confetti-filled convention center a mile away. I can't remember what I wrote, but I felt better after I got it out.

As a friend and I were driving back to Denver from Kansas City, we decided to pick up two of our friends and *keep* driving on to Los Angeles. It was another whirlwind of a trip, and we had a blast. I surprised a girl I had never met in person and we ended up staying at her apartment for a week. One of my friends and I both got stung by stingrays, leaving us in crippling pain for hours.

Back in Chicago, the rest of the year was painful. Since the time I arrived at Moody, I'd had a close friend whom I saw only as a friend for almost two years. One day, I woke up and realized that I was an idiot and she was the most beautiful human being I had ever known. When I confessed this to her, she opted to remain friends rather than pursue a relationship, but I was crushed. Although we were never 'together,' it felt like something deep had ruptured. It took a full year to heal.

The positive result was plenty of poetry and sad songs.

The negative result was learning how to heal from a heartbreak, and having to dwell in that season.

I stayed in Chicago that summer which was also rough. I was working construction, which I hated, and felt like I had so few friends at the time. I found out the hard way that, during the summer, everyone goes home from college. It was a very lonely season.

I got a job in the fall as a rock climbing instructor and, to be quite honest, don't remember many other significant things happening this year. They were overshadowed by a sense of isolation and rejection.

Perhaps the coolest part of the year was starting to volunteer at a ministry in the Cook County Juvenile Detention Center leading Bible studies. I don't know that I've ever seen teenagers so earnestly looking for something—or Someone—to come and lift them up out of their sins; people so hungry for grace. Although it was only once a week, many of the things I saw and heard in that prison will stay with me for a long time...

It's here that You surprise me, trapped in the secret place.
And You walk all over me, like I'm a summer sidewalk.
I'm a small child all alone in a house.
You're healing tissue now.
There's a reason I can pen a dozen lines that
sound good on their own.
But, put an empty novel in my hands and tell me to fill it?
Never.
I'm no Big Picture painter.
Teach me how to love the invisible God again.
Somehow, touching a beautiful girl is easier.

Flowing Like A Stream
1/17/14

I feel like I've finally gotten away.

After three days of driving across the American desert, I escaped the four days spent with her. Escaping California with my body is not the same as escaping California with my mind and my affections. I want these thoughts to be tangible. I wish I could extract them from my head, lie next to them in bed for a while and act like I'm drifting off to sleep. Then, once they have entered their REM cycle, I will suffocate them with my pillows and stab them repeatedly with the butterfly knife I keep in my desk drawer.

I'd wrap them in a whitish translucent trash bag from the dorm lounge and drop them down the trash chute in the storage room.

"How tormenting they were!" I would sigh in relief as I listened to the *ka-shuck ka-shuck* of them falling away from my head and down into the basement dumpster. Those thoughts belong in the darkest damp corner of the blackest midnight train station. A place where you sit in the deep silence of the night, still as death, wondering if you just saw a shadow move.

I keep having visions of tunnels.

When I think about trains, I feel more free. And that darn devil knows that when I start feeling free, I'm coming for him. He best prepare to breathe carpet air.

How do I sort out my feelings for this California girl when I'm trapped in the igloo-ish prison of Chicago? I need her warm soul to come and melt away these bars. She's an athlete; the make and breed I could never aspire to be because I weigh too much.

I still feel pain in my heel where the stingray struck me. I carry this pain as a reminder of the bittersweet pleasure of that road trip to California. Just as the highest climax of human ecstasy milks the deepest wells of our delight hand-in-hand with a pinch of pain, the puncture wound and venom in my heel serves as a squealing hole of happiness with every step I take. It catapults to memory those four days on the West Coast.

A riot rages within me right now. It's the type of riot people attend purely to fight, not because they have something to fight for. I don't know why this riot rages but it's there nonetheless, and it grows more and more impatient. How shall it be resolved, save to invite the all-consuming Fire to come and melt it into peace? A peace as still as death.

I guess I'm still working on dying to myself.

It took all day to wake me up,
come find me, my sleepwalking friend.
I seem to have misplaced my map
while reading the letter you penned.
I think I thought I saw you there,
beneath the west coast sun.
Her winter's warmer temperatures
had hindered our cold fun.
I've seen you drop your groceries,
your eyes were reservoirs.
The dammed up tears became a laugh—
you let me in your door.
I think I see you clearer now,
I've run you through my pen.
Now get some rest, you sleepy head,
new California friend.

I've got nothing new to write
and I've got nothing left to say.
I started looking in the mirror
but my body ran away.

It left my eyes fixated
on the land I left behind.
I tried to look over my shoulder,
but my body took my mind.

So now you've headed out to find me
while my eyes start to erode.
I'd love to help you look, but
I got lost on open roads.

I think my body's driving,
heading west all through the night.
I bet my body's gonna find you,
just to make sure you're alright.

And if you find me, tell me,
'cause I don't know where I've been.
I've gone and slept among the pigs,
blindly delighting in my sin.

Until then, I'll keep looking,
going there, then somewhere else.
I know I'll find You some day,
but first I need to find myself.

I'm sitting in the window seat of an aisle of heavy sleepers. I just finished watching the pink and orange sunset from the *other* side of the clouds. Turns out the sky goes straight from baby blue to midnight black at this altitude.

In the airport earlier, I was thinking about family. I always imagined reaching a point in time where I'd come home to my parent's house and everyone would smile and hug, and eventually my father and I would fall to professional-sounding "grown-up talk." My girlfriend/fiancée/wife would be elsewhere with my mother and grandma and we would embody the Rockwell-esque image of an American family. I've seen that happen in time with my cousins, as they have off and grown up, gotten married and launched families. I always imagine reaching a plane of life in which we congregate and no one fights and no children misbehave and everything goes smoothly as we contentedly absorb the given vacation or holiday visit together.

However, I feel as if today, God gave me a sort of revelatory insight to this, and how I see my family. After spending nearly a whole week with them, I realized a few things. I realized that we are all just exactly who we are. I am not my cousin Ben, or Chelsea, or Samuel, or Tyler. My dad is not theirs, nor is my mom. We Renoes tend to be goofier, less precise and more haphazard. There is no 'Golden Era' of time spent with family.

Everything that has ever happened in my life happened during the *Now.* The trouble is being there when it happens.

My senses have become so numb to visual and audio stimulation that I've forgotten exactly how to alert them to the Here, the Present, the Now. I think in some ways, I was able to return to that place throughout this break. I recall running atop the crest of the dirt hill on that pitstop in Utah. I flung my thrashcoat around my head and whooped and hollered at the top of my lungs as I sprinted to the edge of the breathtaking view. The stone behemoths before us rose like still giants out of the ground. In the other direction, we could see for miles as the enormous expanse of canyon land bared itself to our eyes. The perfectly blue sky was dotted with puffy cartoon clouds and held nothing in that moment but bright promise.

We were healthy. I was healthy. I was in motion, crossing the country with some friends. Living the college spring break dream I had always dreamed of. And though little of it was exactly how I envisioned, I was awake enough to soak in some glimpses of it. Like that midnight we were longboarding around Seal Beach and ended up at the water. Brad coaxed me into stripping down and jumping into the water wearing nothing but my contact lenses. We screamed as Ari and Drew watched from the sand.

It was equally amazing when I swam ashore and spontaneously began running up the coastline. Still nude. I came upon a resting flock of seagulls on the sand, and as I ran through, they all lifted into the air, squawking. There must have been hundreds of them ascending into the darkness. I ran about a quarter mile before the realization dawned on me that if I happened upon another human on the beach, I would still be stark naked.

Naked with no excuse for myself.

Just naked.

And at that point, the other three boys could have absconded hard with all my clothes for all I knew. So I ran the quarter mile back, back through the cloud of noisy gulls, back to where Brad still stood naked in the water, trying to convince Ari and Drew to join him in the brackish tide. We dressed, walked back to the street, and continued boarding, ending up at a huge tree right on the end of Main Street. I climbed the tree and pulled a slug off of it.

I also learned a lot about people on this trip. I learned that no one operates exactly the same and NO ONE operates like me. Everyone has their stuff. When they travel or eat or shop or explore or drive, everyone does it so differently that it's impossible to understand them all. I learned that people are in my life to receive love from me, and to love me back, not for either of us to be used to reach utilitarian goals. I can use people for *what* they can give me, or I can let them give to me of themselves. One will satisfy a short-term desire; the other will produce fruitful, mutually beneficial relationships which honor God and breed life.

I'm a shipwreck sinking outside of the sea,
I'm a wildfire burning down thousands of trees.
They represent people, and their branches are arms,
(but) I skip through the kindling and go for the heart.
They've called me a tower that fell in Siloam,
I crushed the eighteen and then lay there alone.
I'm a bulldozer blowing through dozens of bricks
and if I cared any less, I'd cease to exist.

Oh, We Used To Talk So Much
4/14/2014 aa

Somewhere in the river
is a fish that I can't catch,
she's as handsome as a tuna,
volatile as a match.
She's a dirty dirty blonde
with all the markings of a soul
who never let herself get lost
outside her little fishy hole.

> *(Chorus)*
> Oh, we used to talk so much,
> and oh, what we could have been
> Oh, you make my knuckles bleed
> won't you please come let me in

I thought I caught her once
but then she wouldn't take the bait;
I asked a simple question
and a week had I to wait.
We saw Chicago's underground
beneath a winter's worth of ice,
but like a wise and weathered pike,
she just wouldn't take the bite.

> *(Chorus)*
> Oh, you used to talk to me
> and oh, what we could have been
> Oh, my knuckles bleeding now
> won't you please let me in

And now I think I'm drying out;
I feel my gills fill up with air,
I think that I forgot because
my memory is spare.
It's just a blink of consciousness,
you see, my brain is like a wheel,
always turning, never resting,
never taking time to heal.
This goldfish head and heart
have never lasted long these days,
so I'll return you to the water
and I'll watch you swim away.

(Chorus)
Oh, we used to talk so much
and oh, what we could have been
Oh, you make my knuckles bleed
won't you please come let me in

Oh, we used to talk so much

A Drought
4/29/2014

I could scratch at the deepest recesses of my soul, and the measly bits I scrape up would not suffice as a gift to You. And though Your overwhelming presence rains down like that day I was caught in the mountains, sometimes we're just too dry to feel the drops. I remember running by the lake through the path with trees all around, wiping the water from my eyelashes as it poured down on me. The surface of the mountain pond was in motion as a billion raindrops hit it at once, over and over again.

You surround me like that wall of mist that rose out of the Cape Cod forest as the stillicides fell through the tall green trees in the midsummer storm. The warm wet wetness fell down on us as we bounded across inches-deep mud, rejoicing in the storm's gift. In the stillness, when our legs stopped moving, the battalion of raindrops sounded off across the wood, bouncing off the leaves and falling all around us.

I have never been anywhere as much as I was there that day; I have never been so *inside* of a place and time.

And though I've never been outside the reach of Your arm, I feel like I have wandered off and sniffed the poisonous daisies of my own desires. It is as if the starving spirit within me has chosen to consume the imaginary cakes my childhood friends and I conjured up in our minds, rather than accept the banquet You freely present me. Allow me once again to enter into that sweet communion.

And I found myself parked
in a lost car again
where the weather inside me
won't weather this storm.
You're a hot air balloon
with your sights on the sky,
and I'm squinting below
where the sun hurts my eyes.
I'm an anchor that fell
fast asleep on the ground
where the rope that you severed
would not hold you down.
So I'll whisper goodbye
from the grass where I lay
but you never will hear now;
you're too far away.

And there's a wall that I built
when you first came around.
Built so high you can't climb it,
it touches the clouds.
But you chiseled on through
to the furnace in me
where I'm burning old letters
in attempts to be free.
You jumped on my bellows
and heated the flame
till it hurt when I saw you
and burned when you say
That this fire I've forged
is now out of control
and I've no other choice
but to let you burn slow.

It's a summer when my body is held together by Scotch tape
and when I slice my foot open
kicking some barnacles, I just glue it shut again.
Today I rode a bicycle and jumped off a bridge.
Tomorrow I'll learn how to fly.
You'll be in Europe on a mountain,
I'll be working on my grave,
you'll be going on adventures
while I'm crying like a slave.
I've had seasons before when
my body's held together by tape,
and days upon days in which
I've wandered without sleep.
Today I raced a surfboard on my bike
and you didn't cross my mind.
It's a feat to get away from you
and leave the winter behind.
Snowy Starbucks treks and warm coats.
We left tracks in the virgin snow
deeper than the weight of our boots without knowing it,
and you did the same to me.
You've pressed upon me yourself,
you impressive physician.
Aggressive as you are, I am amazed at how
gently you laid me down.
You stilled my anxious hands
and sang me a song.
You taped up my wounds, and angry as I grew,
I couldn't get you to lower your glue.
You're a healer of men, but you must break them first.
I'll lower my voice when I wake up.
You're a lighthouse, but you're too far from the waves.
I've already broken my vessel in the heat of your light.

5/26/14

We humans are such fragile things
it hardly takes a touch
to tear apart a self we made
and throw it in the dust.

We walk around inside of shells,
our exoskeletons.
And should it break or chip away,
our instinct is to run.

I bought a fancy painted one
from someone we both know.
Its colors were so loud this shield
was quite hard to ignore.

But lo it broke and fell apart
and naked did I stand
without a friend to sit by me
or come and hold my hand.

But in the stillness came a sound
so quiet and so soft.
He asked why I had tried to hide
and run from Him so oft.

Before my lips could even move
or answer fill my mind,
He picked me up and dressed me in
an effervescent shine.

Its beauty never faded and
it wouldn't hide me well,
because it showed me me me me
and wrenched me from my cell.

I enter in the wedding feast
and never have to be
a wanderer from out the fold
of God eternally.

His gentle hands have gathered all
the pieces of my shell
and rendered them quite useless by
deliv'ring them to hell.

6/20/2014

I spent the summer diving headfirst into
red light intersections with
The Kings of the Suburbs,
The Kings of Summer.
We got stranded on the South Side
and biked home naked in the rain.

When the rain dives head first into my skin,
I know the Lord is teaching me something deep.
This loneliness only exists in loud and noisy crowds,
so today it's safe to say I'm glad they're not around.
I dove headfirst into the Chicago river
and have yet to surface.
Holding your breath for this long makes
every one of my broken ribs ache.

6/28/2014

This summer morphed into matter before my eyes.
It was an amorphous blob,
not traveling east or west along a linear timeline,
but escaping the bounds of progression
and crawling up north
or bouncing down south.
Time has frozen, and I with it.

1 Kings 3
7/6/2014

Time stands still in a siege, still,
the waters run
red as blood on a beach, till
they strung him up,
king's son hanging like incense
burnt to the bone,
scared away all the offense;
they're going home.

Summer, 2014

In this pretty city's solitude
I'm killing all my lambs
and this pretty girl I'm talking to
does not know who I am.
I'm living in this timeless state
where I can't see it pass.
I doubt it does and that's because
this week's the same as last.

Dave and I
7/13/2014 ad

We drove to where no people are,
escaped the urban sprawl.
We ran like dogs beyond the hill
to where no phone can call.

This city life has made me ill,
I hope I'm never cured,
'cause I'm in love with mountaintops—
or seas—we can't be sure.

These things that men just love to build
will all soon be decayed.
So Dave and I went to the hills,
a place we should have stayed.

Morning
Summer, 2014

I walked out of the bedroom and saw God seated at the kitchen counter reading the paper.

Crying.

We weren't talking.

Or at least I wasn't.

Nor was I listening.

Hey sister in searching,
do your rooms reek of holiness?
Of a blood-puddled floor,
made slick by the offering?
The holy man smears his face
and grows his hair long,
and gains death.

Show me what you've earned
and I'll show you what I've received.

———————

Spirit follows me, Spirit befriends
Spirit continues where all my strength ends.

———————

I'm on a bus thinking of a girl.
She's a model by the Great Lakes.
I hope that in my broken cisterns
I'm not using her as glue.
A word is a mountain;
a curse a tsunami.
Her lips may destroy
or they just may heal me.
You see the man on the hill?
He reeks of holiness...
or death. We cannot be sure.

Do you know who you are?
Can you walk a mile in your own shoes?
Spend some time in silence
and receive what you lose.

7/26/2014

It smells like smoke,
sweat from every color of skin,
and alcohol
at the dance in the park.
Summer is climaxing and
I've spent half of it dying.
I didn't think I understood You.

Now I know I don't.

I've seen sorrow blended
with salvation
on a dancing black man's face.
I saw sweat roll down
like tears
on the cheek of the old Native.
I brought a robotic motion
to the potluck of movement
in the park this evening.
The floor was fast and ferocious
and we dove on in.

After the human rainbow recessed,
we biked the Loop for a minute,
shooing drivers from their lanes.
Tonight I gazed with anger
at the beautiful face of God.

I'm experimenting with grace.

I breathed in His costly perfume.
It smelled like dancing humans.

8/4/2014 aa

Don't come back to Chicago,
the wind is against you wherever you blow
It shouldn't be this hard to see you.
It shouldn't be this hard to see You.
Now I write what nobody sees,
I carry this pen like a disease.
We rode our bikes through thunderstorms,
and laid some waste to last year's norms.

A young and drunk girl held my hand
while walking back to her hotel.
We found her stranded by the park,
she smelled like weed and alcohol.

I ached while sitting on the curb
and hearing how my friend was beat.
He loved his parents even though
his life was less than bittersweet.

I thought I saw You underground,
I thought I heard You say
that every lesson resurrects
amidst the painful days.
I feel myself maturing now,
in suffering and drought.
I asked You for communion, though
I didn't think You'd shout.

Seven years out and I still remember every single thread in that sweater you wore. You handed me a can of generic brand soda and we went for a walk.

It was the summer I knew myself. It was the summer I lost myself.

I still recall every wave that crashed against those docks while we stood on them, deliberating our relation to each other and to the earth. Where did it go? Why didn't I call you? I know I snapped a picture of you seated on the rail of the dock, but that was two lifetimes ago. That was before I knew the world.

Before we knew the world,
I saw you sitting on a rail.
I held your hand down to the sand
and wrapped you in a sail.
I still remember every sweater
that you wore inside your home.
We walked the tracks and headed back
to our new outdoor home.
Our lips had never touched, you see,
although you knew me well.
And I saw your humility
in stories you would tell.
Now it's been seven years since then,
and I have loved and lost.
And oftentimes, my heart resigns
to longing after docks.

8/9/2014

I'm caught believing
in the dirty Midwest
that You exist.
I had put my hope in a tower.
I'm leaving a wedding
with the wind pouring in
through the open top
and wandering out into
the continent.
Take me as far from this city
as east is from her west.
I never want to lose myself
and wander on accident
into her noisy walls.
Help me to forget

this place.

8/21/14

Will you ever put an end to this tangible gloom,
or am I knocking on the door of an empty room?
I came and sat down just hoping to bleed,
but the giant sits in silence with his quiet disease.
It's a tick who's always talking and he's stuck in my skin,
and I compare him to my bowels, my addiction to sin.
Will you ever lift your hand so that mine can resume,
or does the giant weep alone in an empty room?

I've got a girl on my mind
and my arms at my side
and I'd continue to bleed
but I've already died.
You could say it's unlucky,
you could say it's alright
but don't ever mention
that I never tried.

In a book by the window
I've written inside
that I'm done with this city,
I'm leaving tonight.
You think that I'm bluffing,
a twist of a kite,
but I'll never come back here,
not even in sight.

The love of the loveless;
a lover requites,
but I've never tasted
or known what it's like.
I've made imitations
and candied delights,
but to dine on this feast
puts a heart to the knife.

Now the risk is the trick
that I never got right,
to just step from the ledge
and to fall from a height.
And today as my dark
marches into the light,
my eyes are wide open
watching day turn to night.

8/26/2014 aa

It's a rainy sunny day
and Conor Oberst is preaching to me
through the stereo system.
You hurt me when
I look at you, your face is made of gold.
This unsung game of hide and seek
has really gotten old.
I caught you red-handed
in a white-hot blouse
and khaki pants,
quit burning down my house.

9/6/2014

Well tonight I've got a feeling
that I won't be getting sleep
because the demons inside you look
different than the ones inside of me.
This is the heaviest season
that my body's lifted yet
'cause everything was far away
and time did not progress.
But now you're thinking like a human
and I'm singing like a cloud
because I called to You in thunderstorms
but didn't think You'd shout.

9/7/2014

I can't figure out what to say to You,
there's so much I (try to) keep hidden.
You already know all my secrets,
yet continue asking me questions.
My intention is to love You,
but as You can see, I've failed.
So I'd love to see Your wind again,
come fill these lifeless sails.
I'm trying just to feel You,
but You feel so far away.
So I'm putting words before You,
should You ever come and stay.

I've built myself some boxes
where my battered friends can sit.
But I myself cannot remain,
for I'm a hypocrite.
But mercifully, You've swung your axe
and shattered all my frames.
They did nothing but separate
me from Your loving flame.
I wrote some rules on tablet stones
which could have been my heart.
I tried and tried, though cold and hard,
I couldn't play the part.

See, hearts of stone do struggle to
accept a warm caress,
and so when I had exhausted mine,
You gave me one of flesh.

Where I Met You
2014

I met You in a quiet train station,
silent as the newborn sun,
quiet like a patch of breath.
Your heartbeat filled my ears till
my temples became throbbing gongs.

I have seen You before,

in the lounge on the 96th floor,
or lost in the New England hills.
But tonight I was reminded.
We wandered the Art Institute
with its checkered tile
floors and rouge lockers,
following the sound of singing throats
until we found You.

I saw You again outside
the ice cream shop.
Your hand held a poor paper cup
that rattled
as the snow fell into it.

9/22/2018 ac

You exude something I tasted in a
   dream once.
It's a familiar strength
      pulling me to you.

10/14/2014

It must be nice to know God,
cry the poets in the balcony.
Because the dancers keep on smiling
a hundred yards below.
Prayers in foreign tongues beg
through tears and heavy breath.
There's one in the spotlight
and two on deck.
Walk on over,
sing your songs to the crowd.
you have ten seconds to pray,
but fifteen's allowed.

11/19/2014

I'm aching in a place I can't name,
it's an old familiar sort of pain
but I'm living in this place that's all right
when I drive out into the night.
You're clutching some pieces of me
like a fifty-one majority.
And I'm feeling with a new patch of skin
that's not desensitized to my sin,
but I'm hoping that You love with eyes closed;
the heavenly gaze is what I fear most.
But I'm finding that You do love Your grace;
like a penny heads-down I'm flat on my face
because this work You began isn't done yet.
There's this song that won't let me forget
and it's all written down in my chest,
'cause I've tried it all out and collapsed in Your rest.

11/24/2014

I looked between the covers, where the lovers have their way,
but found that fleeting pleasure never did intend to stay.
I looked inside my pocket for a sum so grand and vast,
but money also robbed me, its fullness didn't last.
I looked out on the mountaintop, and by the sandy coast,
but never did I find the view that suited me the most.
I looked for Love both high and low, but never could I find
a love so deep it covered me and left my past behind.

In all my searching, I did grow to hate this empty life.
It came on me so suddenly like cattle to the knife.
But at the bottom, there I lay, exhausted from my spree;
I never had to look for it, for one day Love found me.
It came to me in silence, when the noise had wandered off,
It sounded like a whisper, coming low and sweet and soft.
My Love said He forgave me, and He made me white as snow,
for mercy conquers sacrifice and glory is my home.

2015

THAT ONE WEEK I WAS FAMOUS

As I continued moving on from my heartbreak, I developed a solid community of friends at Moody, and had two phenomenal roommates (I'm still in love with Andrew and Alec). I finally began to feel nestled in the community, and as is now typical of my life, that's exactly when I wrapped up college and left.

I graduated college and didn't know what else to do, so I returned home to Colorado. Most of my community there had evaporated by that point, dispersing across the country, so I once more entered a lonely season. I slowly began making new friendships and reawakened some old ones.

I met the Middle School director at my dad's church, and I still remember the day we became friends. I left the gym, went to his office in the church and bluntly told him we were going to be friends. And we still are.

Around that same time, I met Rachael, who also worked as an intern at my dad's church, and we hit it off with our weird personalities and obscure tastes. Another day I ran into an acquaintance from high school at the gym, whom I hadn't talked to for five years. Robb and I also started hanging out regularly, and soon I realized that the three of us got along swimmingly. Now, there isn't a day that goes by without the three of us texting, and we have matching Doodlebob tattoos on our calves (see Dedication Page).

I juggled jobs, and there was one solid week where I was simultaneously a bouncer at a bar, a nanny and a construction worker. Two things combined to form a state of millennial stagnation: Not knowing what I wanted to do with the rest of my life, and the lingering feeling that I wasn't yet fully 'grown up' and ready for a real career

(Update: Still not sure if that feeling ever goes away).

In December, I flew back to Chicago to visit friends, and realized what foolish timing it was, as they were all busy studying for finals. For that reason, I went on a run one rainy night and accidentally got world famous for a week. All the attention messed with my head and I thought I was the new Justin Bieber. Agents and publicists from LA were reaching out and telling me I should move out west. So I did...

1/20/2015

Really it's a feeling
in the desert of my head
when I drive on out to Utah
sitting stiller than the dead.
And the weather in my chest
looks like a storm is coming on,
and I'm turning the ignition
and You're turning on the dawn.
I'm walking on a puddle
made of salt and melted snow,
and I'm looking for a God
who's bearing weary sinners' woe.
Really it's a camera
that's poisoning my dreams
by taking something out of something
and it's blurring all the seams.

how to get over anyone

Try this step. Works every time.   Feb. 3rd, 2015

Wait a long,

long,

long,

long,

long,

Long time.

Works every time.

6/20/2015

Inside of the inside of the inside of
New Jersey,
I'm diving into the sea of faces
attached to legs,
arms,
chests,
and hair.
And I long for long hair,
golden in a trickle down the back,
dripping from her head to her
shoulders to the small.
Inside her insides, I've longed
for that soul,
eternal and inconsequential.

To Strong, Re: Julie
9/28/2015
(Written with a migraine in the Berkley Perk Cafe, Boston)

Right now I can't see a thing,
but I'm dying for what you have—
not only sight,
but to be seen.
I see you in the corner of my memory
jumping over a fence,
playing punch cup.
I'd go smoke in the alley
if only to fill my lungs with
the chemicals that exist between you two.
I'm no chemist, but I can see—
even in my blindness—
substances are volatile.
Whether yours are dangerous or beneficial,
only more tests will tell.
You're steering your bicycle through a red light,
don't ever buy a helmet.
You could say I'm not a fan of preventative measures.
You said,
The heart wants what it wants
and I'll stand beside you indefinitely,
bellowing that same earnest chorus.

10/21/2015

It's about time I
chased after something I want.
Something that makes me nervous.
Something I love.

In Australia we caught a lot of birds
in our nets.
They sleep in low trees
but the possums ran away.
They love heights beyond the reach
of our poles,
watched us from meters above
with glowing eyes.

There is no thrill
in catching what comes to you.

It's not about how badly I wanted it;
wanted You,
but how You never really seemed to exist.
Like an invisible boy
observing from the edge,
You walked around the perimeter until You were sure
it was time to get some skin in the game.
I wanted it so badly,
lying in my bed and shaking,
filling my head with longings after dust.

Because what else is a misdirected desire,
but a fistful of a moment?
Open your palm and it's gone.

Now every line feels forced.
Every prayer carefully constructed with a
ruler and a pocket square.
I saw You once in Australia,
or was it Thailand?
And I sang loudly so You'd hear.
Now that You've retreated again to the edge,
(or is it I who closed my eyes?)
I seem to be getting hungry.
Missing You never felt like distance,
it felt like building four walls around myself.

I've been wrung out before but never like this
never till empty and never till dry.

2016

LAX > CHI > DEN

Dave and I were off to Los Angeles! My best friend rode with me all 18 hours over three days in my beat up Corolla to answer the call of celebrity. I think the phrase they used was "sugar talked." All these quasi-high-ranking agents and publicists promised me fame and glory if I only came out to LA, so I did.

And it was…interesting. Suddenly I realized I was in way over my head. everywhere I looked were people who were famous or trying to be. Every barista or waitress was a fashion model, and every man was either a millionaire producer or movie star. In church I would sit next to people who were in Beamer commercials, or the girl who had a line in the *Entourage* film.

And me? I had $400 in my bank account and a viral video people were quickly forgetting about.

I lived in a home with ten other Christian dudes, one of whom became a good friend of mine to this day. Johnny and I became creative collaborators, always pushing each others' ideas and dreams to become realized. That's the thing I missed most about LA: the city hums with electrical creative energy and everyone has a project they are working on or a goal they are working toward.

Without a solid job, and with my moment in the spotlight quickly dimming, I decided to head east to Chicago for the summer. I figured that maybe there's a better chance of something catching on back in the city that made me famous, and once more I was wrong.

Though I got recognized on the street occasionally, I lived in government subsidized housing with several other guys my age, whom I barely ever saw, and most of whose names I cannot remember. It was possibly rock bottom. Lonely, poor and directionless, I hoped that Chicago would revive some of the *joie de vivre* of college and reconnect me with my buds. But when the summer ended and classes resumed, I felt like the creepy old guy hanging around his alma mater because he can't seem to move on.

So I moved on.

I went back to Colorado because my brother was at school in Montana, so his downtown Denver apartment was free. Robb and I moved in and immediately dove into the Denver 'scene' where we were. We loved living together, so we decided to move into a house.

We signed the lease on a 700-square foot bungalow with a giant backyard and threw a lot of parties. The house was 112 year old, though, and she showed her age with weak, squeaky spots and funky quirks. For instance, there was a giant hole in the center of the living room floor with a grate set on top of it.

Robb and I had a blast, daily crafting new inside jokes and hosting friends constantly. Although it was illegal, we also had weekly bonfires in our backyard. Our home became a gathering place for folks, and I slowly entered a new season of enjoying close friends and getting networked into a consistent community where I live...

Once more,
let me inquire of the Lord,
for O! is His silence jarring to my senses!
Ten times ten times ten times
did I call out to Him from the place of my sin.
And every time His answer was the same:
[*silence*]

Yet even more times has His mercy reached my
knees, rising until I drowned in it.
Even more times has He picked me up from my filth,
naked and spent,
unable to hide and too frail to run.

I've run from You,
O Keeper of my salvation.

O, how I have departed!

I have longed for Your death, that I
may take my inheritance now,
impatient son that I am.

But ten times ten times ten times
have you sought me out in the valley of the dead,
taking me from my place of sin
to Your hill of resurrection.

I Ran By The Water
3/2/2016

I ran by the water,
my bare feet slip-slopped atop the wet
sand in between the breaks that rushed in
and splashed my shorts.

I ran by an old Chinese woman,
standing like granite toward the sunset.
I pictured her longing,
longing for the Pacific to unfurl before her
so once more,
she could lay eyes on her home.
I hear the words of the psalmist,
as he strums and whispers,

How can I sing a song of Zion in a foreign land?

So I ask him,

Where have we been
that was not a foreign land?

And I'm still running,
clinging not to this strange country,
but setting my eyes on Zion,
longing one day to arrive and be
an alien no more.

Am I the only one?
3/7/2016

Am I the only one
who feels distant from God
more often than near?

Am I the only one
pretending I've heard His voice?
I would love to catch even a whisper.

Am I the only one
waiting for some kind of revelation
the way a child works on growing all year
until their birthday
and in one moment, passes from
4 to 5?

I'm waiting for my birthday.

Am I the only disciple nodding
off in the garden?

I can't be the only one who
prays memorized words.

Sometimes I think someone swapped out
my glass of resurrection wine
for a box of grape juice.

Experiments in Glory
4/1/16

Forget these temporary pleasures.

Forget the lover's kiss and the gentle pressure of her hand against my arm. Forget the parties, the clothes, and the electrical circuiting in the palms of our hands keeping us alive. Forget the blanket we lay on in that field that cloudy midnight. Culver City was electric. Take me back there and I would spend endless days just dwelling in that feeling.

That emotion.

It's the free fall where your organs elevate within your ribcage, erasing all other places and times, presenting you with only the very raw Here and Now.

I would trade all that for a taste of glory.

For something more intense than a free fall and more intimate than a simple touch. After all, how much nearer can one draw to another than to simply reach out and touch them?

The tragedy of fallen flesh is every touch ends. Each one exists only a fleeting matter of moments before the sun comes up, the lights come on, and the magic escapes. I think every close call I've ever had with glory ended before it could climax. The curtain falls and the actors retreat to the greenroom to rub the stage makeup from their faces.

I touched you in Chicago. I kissed you on the mouth. I pushed the hair from your neck and held you in the dark. But like each close encounter with the infinite, you grew tired and drifted away from me.

Your body was in my arms but you were not.

The mystics in their quiet rooms speak of a glory that visits them in their shiny silence. Sometimes I feel it in the rain. Foreign monks build temples from blood money then reach for glory through the emptying of their minds. Sometimes I've felt it on the road—those silent drives in the dark as the white stripes slip rhythmically beneath the car.

I've never been able to wrap my mind around a God big enough to make All This, so I made idols of women instead. At least I can wrap my arms around them. At least I can hold them for a little while. (Though I always wish it were a little while longer.)

All my life I've been looking for glory.

Hunting it, really.

I remember that rainy day on Cape Cod when I faced You in the forest. We were dressed like Adam and splashing through the mud. The glory was so near, I thought the next raindrop to slap my skin might finally burst the bubble once and for all.

My boys in Chicago and I ran to Lake Michigan because the sky was pouring warm rain. We dove in and listened to the world; silent, save the impact of the drops on the water's surface. Those gentle waves lapped at our chests in the windless afternoon. I was convinced the glory was waiting for us in the mist just a little further out on the water.

But once again, the clouds departed and the rain stopped. The puddles evaporated and we toweled off.

We were so close.

So I didn't see glory when I sat on the bare back of an elephant while we paraded through a Thai jungle. And I missed it again when I played soccer with the Nigerian kids—But I was close! The way you can taste the meal your mother is cooking just by inhaling its scent.

I think that's all this world can be—close.

I think we can only catch a hint of its flavor. Glory eludes us like that phantom in the attic—always calling out our name, then vanishing when we get too close.

The house lights come on, the actors bow then retreat to the greenroom to hang their costumes on the rack.

All this tells me is that glory is somewhere, but it's always somewhere else. Somewhere we can't touch in this life, but we can sniff it out. C.S. Lewis said that we can't attain it on this world, so we were probably made for another one. This world is not all there is.

It tells me I have a home I haven't seen yet, but my name is written on the door of my room.

I've come close to glory several times, but have yet to hold it without it wriggling from my fingers. I've come close, and will arrive there soon.

The Lord is glorious and I draw near to Him. I've chased Him through the trees and sat with Him in silence. I'm longing for glory so I'm binding myself to Him.

He's the best chance I've got.

Escondido
4/2/2016

Take me back to Escondido
I'd like to undo what I've done
Yes, take me back to Escondido
I'd let you know I'm not the one

Nick
5/17/2016 an

I met a friend in Los Angeles
who made a song that made the
whole world nod.
Their toes tip tapped and danced
until 1:51am.
I saw his long fingers pull his
long curls down from his black hat.
       Black shirt
       Black coat
       Black pants
       Black shoes
       I don't know what color his socks were.

Good to be Naked
5/24/2016

He sat me down and said
it's not as much about what she looks like on the outside,
my grandfather told me,
although that is nice,
it's not as much about her suntanned body
as it is
the sunshine that shoots from her eyes
even when she's sixty-six,

he said,
sure sex is great
and a good body is exciting at first,
but eventually,
it's just good to be naked,
it's nice to be naked with the same old person,
my grandpa said,

and some people
think their parents are still chaste
and never *do it,*
but I'm glad my grandparents
are still magnets growing old,
as I hope to be old with someone
too.

Reflections on a Summer Fling
Written 6/8/2017, regarding events from a year prior.

You were, for all intents and purposes, an amorphous mist I tried to cling to as if you could resuscitate my arid heart. We kissed in your sweltering apartment in New York.

"Come over," you said, "but they don't turn the A/C on until later this month, so it's a thousand degrees in my apartment."

You came down to the lobby to let me in. I had driven over instead of biking, despite the warmth of the night, and you assured me I was okay to park there.

You were short and beautiful. Your mediterranean features were high and olive-colored, framed by dark hair which tonight was messy. When you pulled it up into a tight ponytail, you looked like a freaking Persian princess who had become matriculated into the midwestern business world.

Only in hindsight do I realize that you were not very fun, but you did have a certain strong allure.

Like that evening we got caught in the massive downpour, I skipped down the sidewalk rejoicing while you sought shelter beneath the nearest skyscraper that would lend its ledge.

We didn't create this city, we just got caught in the rain and begged its charity. And it was all too happy to oblige. New York was the sprawling metropolis where an atheist and a Christian could meet in a Chipotle and initiate a summer fling.

That night you cautioned me repeatedly that you were gross and had been poolside all day without a chance to clean up. I assured you I preferred the natural look of your skin.

The sharp ledges of your lips drew me in, with their gentle curves and pointy corners. The way your cheeks softly folded over them into a dimple spelunkers wouldn't dare to disturb. I began to wonder, sitting in the chair next to the couch where you sat, why you would allow me into your space. Into your apartment. Into your home. And why there were no better suitors found to fill your sheets this evening.

You told me you stopped believing in God because He just kind of stopped mattering. You simply realized that He didn't exist anymore, the way one realizes they only got 11 chicken nuggets in their box for 12.

For you, God was nothing more than numbers that didn't add up.

I told you about how Jesus is, like, everything, and there is nothing beyond Him. Zoom out far enough and you always get to Him.

But I was zoomed in. I was focused on the sharp slivers of your eyelids as they rested above the dark irises as you examined my visage. I was talking about God but you were studying me.

"I need to go home so I can shower," I announced. "Got an early morning tomorrow."

"I have a shower," you lowered your eyes, dead serious. "And you know what's here that your house doesn't have?"

"You have a steam shower??"

"No…me. I'm here."

My stomach twisted into a complex knot of premature guilt and intense desire. I imagined your small, tan body pressed to mine while we stood in the tub. To accept would be to break a barrier from which there is no retreat.

"What if we were just friends?" I asked. Deep inside my head I plotted out how I would befriend you, continue these lengthy talks on religion and God until you finally caved and asked Jesus to come live inside of you, and I could properly woo you, wed you, and follow you behind that shower curtain. But that was at least…seven months away.

"I could never be friends with you," you stated bluntly. "I would just want to make out with you all the time."

I thought for a moment.

I moved from the chair toward you, into an awkward crouch-slash-bend over the edge of the couch.

And I kissed you.

Your lips were the exact right elixir of soft and firm. They were possibly better than expected. Not only were they phenomenal to the touch, but they left the most delicious tang on my own lips. Not a manufactured fruity taste, but a very human flavor. The kind you would imagine if you were to try to conjure what an exotic woman tastes like.

I knew in the back of my mind that kissing atheists was wrong.

"Wasn't expecting that," you said, authentically surprised.

I can't remember what exactly was said in the following minutes, but I ended up seated directly in front of you on the ottoman. We faced each other and spoke closely. Our knees touched. My hands held your elbows and I noted how soft the skin on your arms was.

We kissed more.

You told me I was bad, but you would help me get better.

"Just do less," you said in a low voice. "Let me…"

You kissed me again. And to this day it was the greatest kiss I've ever had.

And when I'm honest and alone, I miss the nearness of your skin. I miss the red warmth of your sunburnt shoulders and the naturally succulent tang of your lips.

And you know what? I'm afraid. That's what good kisses do; they put a little bit of fear inside of you.

Fear that, when this one doesn't work out—which it won't, our religious differences have made sure of that—I'll never have another kiss like that. Perhaps the next girl's lips will be too smushy, or her flavor won't be like yours. Fear that, when I do meet the right one, her body will be all wrong and maybe she won't put her hair up into that sleek black ponytail like yours.

I've had dreams since then that I stayed longer. That I spent the night and woke up holding you. But I didn't. After the third or fourth round of kissing, I stood up and departed. We both knew it was over. We both knew it never had been.

I remember turning to talk to you in the doorway, said something about moving a mattress you wanted to get rid of, and was off. We both knew I'd never be back for that mattress. No kiss goodbye. It was over the moment we rose from the couches. We both knew it, and to this day I still wonder if it ever did exist.

Ontologically, I can't help but wonder if we are different, you and I. Is it more than a line on a form that segregates our religious differences, or is it more? Is it more like the difference between apples and a 10 million tonne glacier floating lonely in the Arctic?

I kissed you, but what was it? What was that substance-less thing we held between us like a child passing water from one hand to the other as he sits in a pool? The thing about trying to hold water is it runs quickly and before you know it, you're sinking your hands beneath the surface again to scoop up more.

You left me thirsty.

Because that's the thing about substance. It is satiating. It doesn't leave you wanting like a burrito made of celery.

You were beautiful but you left me wanting.

Ours was a relationship made entirely of negative calories.

Ours was a kiss that reverberates through a thousand punk rock songs but will be forgotten in the High Country to come.

When everything is shaken and only the unshakable remains, that night in your apartment will be lost in the dusty annals of trivial—but pleasurable— mistakes. And I am eager to consume something substantive once more.

The Atheist
6/5/2016 ag

Now we're really going somewhere,
yes we're really moving then.
The little rabbit has a hole
although it doesn't have an end.
He's a fluffy little guy
with a curious puffy tail,
but the nest he's looking for,
it doesn't take him anywhere.
He doesn't know he's wagering
what heaven knows you must,
his little twitchy nose
simply departs with every gust.

We're really moving now,
I see the future setting in,
and you can deny it all you want
but every tunnel has an end.
I saw a rabbit running wild,
he was twitching with the fleas,
although he didn't believe in them,
he had inhaled their disease.
His mind was nothing more than
just a stubborn bit of mush,
and every quiet veterinarian
this little guy would hush.

We're heading a direction
and we're gonna get there soon,
although your eyes see only darkness
and your phone says it is noon.
You're just a fluffy little rabbit
and you're hopping through your hole
but the darker night is coming
where you gain or lose your soul.
I wish that I could be a rabbit
and I'd show you to the ground,
just like Plato or Saint Augustine
who knew what he had found.

7/26/2016

If currency's material to
which the people assign worth,
then surely fame gives people head and tails
though coins had done it first.
What does the emperor look like?
Where is his image cast?
Is it not in the pocket of the peasant,
a symbol that will surely last?

So how about I assign some worth to You,
and turn my penance into coin?
Am I not enough to ratify
this longing in my loin—
Can I escape the dreaded scale
which measures out my good?
I feel like knowing You should satisfy
'cause others say it should.

It pushes me to feeling You,
to scratching up my chin
because my wallet's running empty
and there's not much else within.
Not the leather in my pocket,
but the prayer-buck in my soul
isn't buying much of anything,
it's like my spirit wore a hole.

I Prefer A Theology
8/10/2016

I prefer a theology whose hair you can run your fingers through while stars shoot overhead.

I prefer a theology that sits on the sidewalk with a McDonald's cup in its hand, waiting for you to reach into your pocket and find a crinkled bill.

The one that gives blind people colors and deaf people song.

Because there are too many theologies that enjoy distance and ask you for some space. Or others that merely sit in rooms and talk about economics. And memorize things.

But I prefer the theology whose makeup runs when she cries over yet another orphan.

The one that pulls your hair behind your ears when you're drunk (again), or holds you after looking at porn (again) because it loves you as you are, not as you should be.

A theology that sells everything (including the car and phone) so that God doesn't seem as far away. A theology that's dependent.

I don't really like a theology that lives in the past. The one that tells me 'God *could have* done this or that…' A theology of scales and balances and measures.

I prefer a living theology over a dead one.

So I guess I prefer Jesus over theology.

I want to contain you.
I want to bottle you up like a concentrate
and drink you in the morning to wake up
and again for an afternoon pick-me-up.

I'd carry you with me everywhere
and feel safe knowing you're in my pocket.

But I can't contain you.
You can't be contained.
To contain you is to kill you
and
I would rather watch you fly away
than to contain you for myself.

She is Cartesian.
She is composed of thoughts.

Dear G,

I never stopped thinking about you, I just started thinking It wouldn't work out between us. Forgive me for dreaming so small! I miss you a lot. I miss Brasil a lot. It's strange to think that after 25.5 years of life, I have only spent one week with you; that's one 1,326th of my life!

Tell me what you're doing now! What were you doing in Africa and Italy?? If I remember correctly, some of your family is Italian? What do you want to do with your life? If you could do one thing with the rest of your life, without worrying about money, time or failure, what would it be?

Lately I have been watching some of my favorite films and they have been igniting within my soul a desire for adventure and travel. Last night, I watched my favorite film of all time, *The Brothers Bloom,* and it was like having gasoline poured on the flame. In one scene, Bloom is talking about his work as an antique dealer and he says, "We saw the dealers who were selling us the antiques coming from exotic countries around the world…The air would be like before a rain—the ions would line up and you could just smell midnight trains to Paris and steamer ships and Calcutta bazaars…"

Don't you want that? Midnight trains to Paris and Calcutta bazaars? I see things like these and they make me long for more than what I've been doing with my life. I have been wasting away in coffee shops and going through the same tired motions as every other American. I finished college and have no real job—all my money comes from writing. In other words, I have no reason to stay in one place. I should be GOING! I should be out and seeing the world! I should be on that midnight train to Paris! Do you want that too?

If you do, let's get started! I have always sought just that one person to be with me on my voyages around the world. One person to share in the adventures. Is that you? It's impossible to tell right now. We need to spend more time together! We should talk more.

When I remember you, I remember a hilarious girl dancing around like a dinosaur. I remember drawing you a picture and writing you an apology song. I remember that night in Brodowski when you put your head on my shoulder and told me you were sad. At the time, I didn't know why, but Lucas told me later that it was because I was leaving the country soon. If I had known sooner, things may have been different! Perhaps we would have had more time together!

I'll wrap it up here and look forward to your reply!

Perilously yours,

ER

P.S., Come to Colorado!

10/24/2016

Look!
How the blood runs down the legs of the Divine
and drips from his toes.

Look!
There he hangs,
more real than the break of day.
The dirt in his shadow
is pooling with his blood.

Look!
There on that hill,
the God-man who borrowed
my sins from me
and does not seem intent on
giving them back.

Look!
There they all go,
my shame and my showmanship,
my darkness and death,
my worry and want.

And Look!
There he is three days later
with holes in his heels
and life in his hands.

A Millennial Hymn
12/8/2016

I have learned that the best thrift stores
cannot be Googled, Bing or Yelped;
They're spread by word of mouth
without requesting Siri's help.
I have learned a plastic zip tie
holds my hood shut while I drive
across the states in my Corolla
just to feel some more alive.
I've learned that cops don't let you trespass
just "to get a better picture,"
and that nine times out of ten,
I'll feel remorse after I've kissed her.

Because I've learned that people come and go—
or maybe I'm the one who's leaving,
always packing up a bag because it's better over there
...so I'm believing.

I've worked a half a thousand jobs
and I've made almost that much money,
and I'll make light of just how broke I am
even though it isn't funny.

I can't name every president,
but I'm fluent in memeology,
and I'd probably be richer
if I'd not studied theology.
Yet here I sit, broke af
and borderline content.
I'm loving what I'm doing
though it won't make me a cent.

12/14/2016

I remember sitting on the Southwest flight and thinking about death. I had been doing a lot of thinking about the next life and what exactly the Bible teaches about it. I have arrived at a place (mostly thanks to N.T. Wright) where I don't believe in a spiritual version of an ethereal 'heaven,' but rather the resurrection and restoration of all things as all of creation follows in the footsteps of the Firstborn of Creation, Jesus Christ. So as I waited for my flight to finally be overtaken by turbulence and go down, like I've always feared with every bump in the air, I penned the words I want on my tombstone on the airplane napkin. Okay, I went through several napkins first...

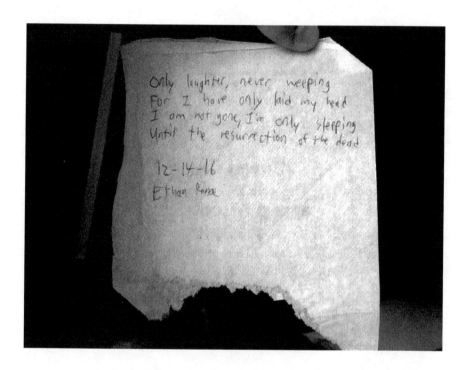

Only laughter, never weeping
For I have only laid my head.
I am not gone, I'm only sleeping
until the resurrection of the dead.

Feeling Bad For Myself At A Wedding
12/17/2016

It's almost Christmas in America
and I'm preparing in the heat.
I'm down below the Carolinas
in Florida's 81 degrees.
And now my roommate's getting married,
I see the leaves begin to fall.
We singles shiver on the tree branch
until none remain at all.

It's just me up here turning brittle,
awaiting snow to take me home.
This year's been colder than the others
and it ends with me alone.
But this is nothing new here,
it's just another year now nearer;
I find a poem everywhere I go
and they help me see a little clearer.

I'm the last dinosaur left living
when all his friends began to die
because I'm watching all my friends go
to that land of You And I.
I'm on a hill beside the river
and there's a party 'cross the side,
and maybe someday I'll go join them,
no longer lonely in the night.
I plan the future by my past
and this humid night reminds
that one more trip around the sun
may leave these lonesome thoughts behind.

I remember the late nights at Moody heading North a mile to the 24-hour Starbucks. The train ride would usually take as long as walking because the Brown Line ran so infrequently late at night unless you caught it at just the right time. I remember Lila Carvell and I making the trek more times than I can count, though it was probably fewer than my brain conceives, because the mind has a way of painting infinite layers over a few small events, making the quality compensate for the quantity.

The mile went fast or slow, depending on the night. Perhaps the distance itself was fluid. Perhaps it depended on the company I walked with. Lila made all time fly by. I remember many days with her, wasting time in coffee shops, supposedly doing schoolwork but talking instead. I don't know why a beautiful, creative, and curious mind like her put up with me, always talking about myself, while she was always, *always* interested in others.

It's hard to find anyone to match her level of energy, creativity, and most of all, her curiosity. I think the thing I miss about her the most was her curiosity. Hanging out with curious people makes the world burst into fitful life, endlessly entertaining and always unraveling new mysteries.

To those who have the world figured out, the world is bland, redundant, and tiresome, as if you're watching a film you've seen a dozen times and you're just waiting for it to be over. But to the curious, it's exciting. You're turning a page and you have no clue what the next one contains, what you'll learn from it or experience on its canvas.

Lila was curious about me. She wanted to read what I wrote—my stories and poems—and I was excited to share them with her. Just like tonight, as I write these things down in my favorite late-night coffee shop in Denver, I'm thirsty for someone to pick up this page and pore over these words with the same intense curiosity.

Tonight I just wanted to write something. Something that may or may not be read by anyone else, but the fact that I created it stands. So I'm pulling from the ever-present alphabet and arranging these guys for you, whoever you are.

Perhaps all creativity is a quest to not be forgotten when we're gone. To say, Look, I made something that will be read when I'm gone. Look, I'm not really gone.

Perhaps all creativity is a battle for immortality.

The thing I realized about my blog posts as of late is that they have become far too formulaic. I get an idea and lay it out in the same pattern and the same level of intensity: that of a baby canary.

But tonight, I'm creating a new formula. It's a free-form formula, like that category of math that uses letters instead of numbers. It's a formula that doesn't look like math because really it's not, and this post is more of me sitting here and slicing my stomach so my innards can pour out before you onto this page. Or screen.

There is another point I remember in Chicago.

There were times in my life when I would look at actresses like Emma Watson and wonder if it were possible for me to find someone as beautiful as her. But then one night, when I watched the movie *Noah* seated beside Lila, I saw Emma Watson on the screen and thought *meh*. Because I looked next to me and suddenly saw someone so much more interesting, so much more curious, so much more beautiful than any distant A-lister on a screen.

What can a 2-dimensional character offer me that's better than a 4-dimensional relationship with another human being? How much more tangible is the girl sitting next to me in seat H6? Look at the way I can ruin her night with one word, or make her feel like a billion bucks with a different one! Look at how I could reach out and touch her nose if I wanted.

I feel like in some ways, I have retreated back to that place of longing for distant two-dimensional actresses and models because there is a hunger and thirst for artificial beauty. Because I haven't been touched in a while.

Look at the way a man can touch a tree, a brick, or a computer and feel nothing. Look at how a woman touches her light switch, her carpet, and her tabletop, and feels no attachment.

But watch the two of them touch. Watch her calf touch his under the table of a crowded restaurant and the entire night shifts. If it's the first touch of a relationship, it's a rush, like cracking open the lid of a chest discovered underground. If it's a familiar touch, there is comfort in it, like the smell of your house when you return for Christmas.

There is value in skin touching skin. Solomon wrote in Ecclesiastes that a man who lies alone will grow cold, but two who lie together remain warm. Skin is unlike any other surface. It's dynamic and raw. It flinches and it slides over bones. It bends and it's warm. It smells both good and bad and in many ways, the feeling of it is what all of us are after. Touch from fathers who didn't hold us when we were younger or mothers who misused their skin against ours. I don't know what this is like, but I know something of the deprivation of touch. Of wandering the world like a passing thunderstorm; it's looked at and talked about, but never really touched.

Skin is a nice thing.

I'm sitting in this coffee shop watching a girl run her boot along her lover's leg. Even through shoes and jeans, it seems like human touch is enough to melt men made of even the strongest of materials.

I don't know why I sat down and wrote this today, nor did I know where it was going when I began. It feels like the night I sat on top of a skyscraper drinking wine and writing poetry with Lila. She inspired things in me I haven't felt in a while but hope to again. Sometimes I wonder if maturity is some kind of letting go of these passionate feelings and settling down into routine and mundanity.

I hope not.

I hope God was more creative than that when he crafted men and women in His own image. I imagine that the Creator is exactly that: Creative. And therefore I must conclude that, if we are made in His image, we are meant to have nights like these. Nights wondering about the world and where the next turning of the page will take us. Of what we will learn and who we will be when the page turns again.

There's no way to know; the only possibility is to fill up the page I'm on with the best possible combinations of words. So here it is: A post I've created for no other reason but to leave something here, like a footprint which lasts longer than I will, but ultimately, as language and syntax march on and are forgotten, will blow away with the eroding of the world.

It was fun while it lasted and I enjoyed this particular string of metaphors.

Hope you did too.

2017

HOW TO HAVE A HOME

Immediately after signing the lease on the bungalow in 2016, I felt a pang of remorse, as if I had just resigned the rest of my life to a settled life along the outskirts of Denver, sedentary in the same city and getting old and boring. I was working as a youth pastor at a small church and absolutely loved my kids (I always referred to them as 'my kids,' never 'my students' for some reason). I loved them so much that I dedicated my second book, *The New Lonely*, to them, and know they'll always hold a significant weight in my heart.

I wrote *The New Lonely* at the end of 2016 and released it in March of 2017. It somehow peaked at #1 on Amazon in the prestigious "Christian Relationships" category and held that spot for two weeks.

That summer, I was asked to be a judge for a national beauty pageant, so I was flown to Orlando for a very surreal weekend. The judges on the panel were: One of the guys who helped launch reality television and now runs his own modeling agency; a former Miss America; Miss South Carolina; a winner of the show *Big Brother*...and me. To put it lightly, I was wildly out of place. The weekend ended up being a blast, however, and I even dated a girl I met there for a little while afterward (Spoiler alert: she broke my heart).

The rest of the year was a steady combination of enjoying living near my family and close friends, every coffee shop in Denver, Roommate Robb (who wrote the foreword for *The New Lonely*), and learning how to do real ministry with real people...

6/29/2017

I see us rising early,
drinking plain black hot coffee,
trying to run for the train
and take State to Milwaukee.
On that day we'll move faster
than all else alive
and we'll breathe out our ghosts
when it's quarter to five.

I picture love in the evening,
it's all warm and red,
but when I crave deep affection,
I see morning instead.
It's the crispest of air;
it's the quiet of dawn.
it's the intimate convos
we've postponed all along.
So I hope that you'll meet me
when the sun breaks the night
and you'll give in quite easy,
won't put up a fight.
Because I want to hold you
while the moon slowly retreats
and we're riding the L
above morn's empty streets.

Your head was nestled under my cheek. How did we fit together? Did we?

Two strangers tangled up in an airplane row. Out the window, we couldn't find the place where the land stopped and the sky began.

It was tangled up in the clouds and colors blurred and faded into a greenish haze. A single tear fell from your eye and I had never seen one shed so precisely. What were you looking at? Or perhaps more importantly, what film played on the projector screen of your mind?

Was it him?

Am I drawn to *you* or simply things about you? Is there a difference? (Yes.)

Do you inspire in me poetry or lust?

I cannot speak but to sing the praises of my beloved.

We sat with our faces inches apart and I wish you would have believed me when I told you how beautiful you are. That man, he did a number on you, didn't he? Today I held America's Last Top Model as she cried on an airplane and her curly hair touched mine.

7/16/2017 at

You said don't get too close—
the butterfly wings are easily damaged.
Don't break them.
You've been broken before
& know how it feels.
Let me save up my emotion for 8 years
and pour it into that hug goodbye,
the one where I felt your
nails on the back of my neck—
small kinesthetic signals. Received.
Whoever lives inside your cell
trying to escape:
Touch my back again
and I'll set her free. I'll let her out.
Today we watched a worm crawl
into his chrysalis.
Tomorrow we'll watch him fly,
pretty
natural
free.
Let's crawl into this cocoon called distance
and see what beauty flies out.

But I can't pull you out.
I have to wait
for you to climb out on your own.

Rain: A Therapeutic Memoir
7/19/2017

The swell of clouds rode into Dennis, Massachusetts that afternoon like a demon tangled in a little girl's white dress. Today I realized that almost all of the best days of my life involve being caught outside in the rain. I think it's something about the atmosphere shift that illuminates the previously arid world we once inhabited. It used to be sober.

Derek and I sprinted from his car to the outdoor patio of a seafood place in this tiny surf town. Earlier that day I had sprinted along the coast as the clouds gathered opposite the sand bank protecting the shore. There was a shark watch at the time, but I saw the heads of seals bobbing in and out of the water, so I knew it was safe to dive in at the end of my run.

Today I'm working on an exercise given me by my counselor which delves deep into my past and the highs and lows in the life of Ethan Renoe. It's simultaneously really hard and beautifully illuminating. Some of the memories are hard to revisit because they introduced a painful belief or a longsuffering wound. Others ache to call to mind because of how beautiful and pure the moments are and I long to return to them with everything inside of me.

But I can't. Time only moves in one direction and I'm caught in her cruel current.

The summer of 2012 was easily the highlight of my life. It was the summer I was homeless on Cape Cod and living on the beach working as a stand-up paddleboard instructor. I had no car and no home. Every day was as fresh and exciting as the sunrise spattered across the morning sky. I didn't even have a smartphone yet, so my mind was yet unadulterated by constant updates and anxious scrolling. I have very few pictures from this summer despite how beautiful the entire season was (The picture above is one of the few saved on my flip phone).

There was the day Bita and I were showing her friend's cousin around and once again the warm rain struck. We had driven quite a way to find a ridiculously long dock which you could jump off at several spots.

One of my favorite things in the entire world is jumping off of things into water. (Even when I happen to kick a barnacle)

It was the end of July, as it is now, and we were caught in the warm rain, springing from the falling droplets into the brackish Atlantic; the tide was barely high enough to dive into the bay and we carelessly threw ourselves in.

Later, after driving back toward the mainland, we stopped at a path I'd wandered many times growing up. Today was different though. The woods were silent save the rain hitting leaves and the mist rising around the trunks of the trees.

The three of us were dressed in swimsuits and took off through the mud and puddles, dashing barefoot through the wet woods and experiencing a very surreal moment.

Then there was the rainy day in Thailand we walked past the trees draped in orange priest robes to reach the giant white Buddha resting atop the mountain.

The same happened years later when a storm rolled into Chicago and some boys from my dorm and I ran to the lake to see the gray sky penetrating the gray waters. Rain has a way of making even the busiest cities fall silent beneath its droplets. We dove into Lake Michigan as it was being broken up by the falling water.

Even years after that, I returned to the same lake during a midnight thunderstorm with my best friend. We ran barefoot through the city's streets, even diving into the lake as it was being struck by lightning. (Not the best idea, but a heckuva rush)

The rain makes me feel alive.

There's something messy about it, but at the same time cleansing.

It's paradoxically peaceful yet active.

It's vibrant but gray.

Rain is a singular thing made up of billions of things.

I'm teaching through Genesis for a few weeks at my church, and Rain is an interesting character in the book. Chapter 2 tells us that prior to the flood, rain never fell on the ground, but rather, streams rose up from the ground.

This is awesome because it makes Noah seem even more crazy to the people around him, telling them that water will fall from the heavens and flood the earth. Because that had literally never happened before. Knowing that gives new shape to the amount of faith Noah had when God told him a flood was coming. It's one thing to hear that rain is coming that will flood the world; it's another entirely when rain has never fallen from the sky before!

And when the rain does come, the Hebrew says that "the floodgates of the heavens were opened." Put yourself in the shoes of a Hebrew several millennia ago: You have no idea what the sky is, what clouds are, or how far up anything is. You don't know what the sun or moon is, nor do you know that stars are the same as the sun, just further away.

Suddenly all these things vanish and water starts to fall.

Like it does today.

To this day, the floodgates of the heavens still open and refresh us and bathe us. The water grows our crops and quenches our thirst.

Little pieces of heaven still fall on us, renewing our world and reminding us that there is peace in the chaos and stillness in the commotion.

One droplet of rain won't flood the earth or change your life, but a collection of many billions will. And it is the chorus of raindrops that moves us and stills us. It is this gathered water that transports me back to that bay off Cape Cod or the Thai mountaintop.

When the floodgates of heaven open, pay attention.

Maybe it's just me, but crazy things happen when we find ourselves caught in the rain. There is an enormous amount of freedom in letting go of your kempt and dry conditions and letting yourself run free, letting yourself be washed and allowing your skin to drink in the water.

Perhaps your preferred method of communing with the Transcendent is something else. Maybe it's snow, books, motorcycles, or stargazing. Whatever it is, pay attention. The Lord is vast and imminent. He is both incredibly far and unutterably close. For me, the rain is something that brings the heavens down to earth and reminds me of the nearness of God.

What's yours?

Today I am sad.

Heartbroken, but to a lesser degree. You were a movie star and I was a teenager with a dream. I held you on an airplane and kissed you in the rain, but our love was nothing more than a cinematic highlight reel without the substance of intimacy. Perhaps I always had my doubts. Perhaps my mind craved a poetic lifestyle more than it did authenticity.

I really really liked you.

I still do.

I find myself becoming angry, but that is more as a result of not being able to be sad for very long. Anger is a secondary emotion and right now I feel more sad than anything. Not sure what to do with that. With this. With you.

I've never understood people who can like someone yet feel nothing for them. As if their desire is unmatched by their....desire? How?

It's as if the art of liking someone is a skill you've yet to master. I'm great at it. I can fall in love with nearly anyone, just watch.

When Robb and I first moved into our home, it was completely empty. We made a dozen trips from our respective homes to lug all of our belongings into it, but because it's an entire house and we made one small car trip at a time, as soon as everything was put away, it virtually made no difference. It was almost like we weren't bringing anything into the home at all because it was so large and our belongings were so small.

Like eating with a tapeworm.

Or pouring water into a holey bucket.

Or like pouring love into you.

No matter how much I encouraged you and poured into you; no matter how many letters or songs I wrote you; no matter how many flowers or coffees I bought you, they all went to waste. They all went into you, absorbed into your blood with little to no effect like a placebo pill.

Perhaps that's all I was; a placebo which did not induce the desired result.

We could have had so much fun.

Oh, we used to talk so much
and oh, what we could have been...

8/10/2017 at

Hang on, let me sit in this sadness,
it feels rough against the soul.
I can't quite seem to shake you off yet
cause in my heart you left a hole.

I know that it'll heal eventually
but there's something I've gotta say.
I know that you will never read them
but I've got to get these thoughts away.

I peaked in the summer of '17,
is it all downhill from here?
I kissed a movie actress
and now I'm filled with fear.

Because a good kiss will always shake you,
always leave you wanting more,
always drill into your chest there
it'll shake you to the core.

There was something in that moment,
it was real and quiet and soft,
I felt you as we breathed in each other,
felt your lips and teeth and mouth.

(The rain hit the windshield and the radio was on,
I tried to recollect the moment, but the song still slips my mind.)

I always thought it would be more,
that this moment would be higher,
that no one wanted what I's selling
till that day I found a buyer.

And you were smiling as you leaned in,
as you touched my arm and chest,
as your fingernails tapped lightly
on the lower back of my neck.

You filled me with a courage
that I haven't felt in years
and now that this is really over
I'm returning to the fear.

But love, don't leave me hanging,
it's best to simply close the door
And I won't wait on empty promises
Because I've heard those lies before

I guess I'll find another you,
another woman good and strong,
though I know it won't be easy,
I looked for you so long.

I guess I'll find another you,
but it's not an easy task.
I know I brought myself to kiss you
I's so timid I had to ask.

I guess I'll find another you,
but one who'll read all of my words.
Perhaps you weren't so awesome after all,
maybe that's what really hurts.

I guess I'll find another you,
Maybe I'll sing until you've gone.
I've just got to get this out of me,
I hope it won't take long.

Because maybe you just won a crown,
and maybe that's not you.
Perhaps the girl beneath the wig
is more disguise than true.

Because what I saw was just a pool,
a shadowy reflection,
and in my mind I pictured you
a photo of perfection.

I know you said that you were bad,
not strong or beautiful,
but what I saw I know I loved
and wanted in the full.

I hope some day you'll find a love
who treats you like I tried,
but I just hope you find this soul
before your own has died.

Old Enough
9/9/17

Passed the point where they ask me for X's on my hands,
reached the point where he apologized as he draws on my wrists.
Sorry I have to do this,
he said with the felt tip in his fingers.
Sorry 'cause I know you're old enough.
Sorry 'cause I see you forgot your I.D.
Sorry 'cause you're growing hair in more places
and your skin is creasing and folding.
Your bones are creaking and your muscles atrophy.
Sorry for the age I can see under your eyes
and sorry that they've seen more than mine now.

Sorry you forgot your I.D. because I can see the things you've seen.
I can see the bags beneath your eyes
are holding more than they did
when I had to check your plastic for your birthday.

The bartender poured me a Coke from
one of those handles with the buttons,
I thought you seemed old enough,
those X's suggest that you're younger than you look.
but you don't look young.
I can see how your skin folds here,
more weathered than smooth.
I can hear how your voice seems weighed down more than
it once was when the inflection peaked higher
and the jokes poured more readily.

Sorry I can't serve you
what you've been drinking for 5 years now.
Sorry I can just give you Coke,
though she doesn't know I prefer it to spirits.

Sorry you're old enough to look like you're old enough.

2018

THE UNFINISHED YEAR

Well, we're just about there.

We're almost at a good stopping place.

You've caught me in the present moment and I hope you've enjoyed getting here as much as I have (though hopefully it didn't take you ten years like it did for me).

This year has been a mellow roller coaster ride. It's about half over, so I can't quite sum up the year in its entirety, but so far it's been a season of change and expectation. If I lived in one place all of last year, this year has already quadrupled that number. I don't know where I'll be come August, much less next year.

So far, I've continued working as the youth pastor to my kids and enjoying a relatively relaxing season. This book descended upon me like a demon in the night (as they always do) and all I've wanted to do is write it. Then compile it. Then edit and revise it. I spent the cumulation of days under my piles of old notebooks, reliving old memories and teleporting through time.

This season is a season of expectation as well. Several friends have gotten married this year, and life shifts. I have accepted a contract to live in Guatemala and teach English and Bible, so for the foreseeable future, that's where I'll be.

Come down and say hi if you want...

The Shape of my Father
3/3/2018 ad

I have seen the shape of my father
hunch and round out
as the years mistreat him
(the days are evil).
I've watched as his joints grow sore
and his surgery count soared
and he flips from father
to grandpa in the batting of an eye.

But yesterday I watched as he
and my mother
ding-dong ditched the neighbor kids,
leaving gumballs on their doorstep.
I watched them fleeing the
scene of the crime
as fast as their achey joints could carry them,
sprinting,
jumping over rock beds
and shrubbery,
laughing loudly together.

I don't want to be the shape
of a grandfather,
but I want my soul to be
the shape of my dad's.

I used to be so patient,
I used to wait so long.
I used to just be torn apart
by every lyric of a song.

I once thought I was perfect
and once thought I was strong.
I used to have enough to eat
until your lips had come along.

I thought that I was gentle
but I must have read you wrong
because we hit it off so chemically
on that night I met your mom.

Now I wonder if I screwed up,
if I let you go too soon,
if this ache that I've been feeling
would be healed by holding you.

You were wild, fun and witty
and I'll likely never know
if we should have kept on moving
by the midnight TV glow.

I like the shape of you; I'm drawn to the curve of your cheekbones and the sway of your hips but there's no way to tell if I love the shape of your soul. Does it swing like your lower back and does it shine like the blue hue of your eyes?

What do you do with a burgeoning universalist who's trying to figure herself out, trying to find this holy God and define His edges?

I once saw the border of the Lord. It was a rainy day on a Buddhist mountain. Thailand was a blur, my memory of that day is streaked like the camera lens with all the raindrops resting on the lens.

The beauty of the day pierced me like your eyes.

You asked me a question with the s's hissing through your teeth, a microscopic lisp and I don't know how I feel about it. I wonder if you're good at asking questions; if you know how to laugh, or if you're a competitor to the core.

You were a notification on my screen, now you're someone I've had a conversation with.

But perhaps you'll help me ask questions. Perhaps you'll beg of me questions which I often fear to ask; questions which scare me because the answers would mean a shift of paradigm, or a broadening of my understanding of the Holy. I'm the one with the freaking circle and square tattoo on my arm, yet I'm the one endlessly crafting boxes where I can store my convenient little god.

If this thing ends up working out
then I'll be happily surprised.
I knew it had potential there
when I was looking at your eyes.

If this thing ends up working out
I know I'll hurt you 'fore it's through.
I know I'm not a perfect man,
but hate the thought of scarring you.

If this thing ends up working out
I'll have to lower all my guards.
You'll get to see that parts of me
are fractured or in shards.

If this thing ends up working out
I swear I'll kiss you every day.
I wanted to so bad tonight,
but wisdom bade me wait.

If this thing ends up working out
we've got a long, long way to go.
But joyful will I be to no more
walk this road alone.

3.14.2018 ae

I've filled up journals and notebooks
so one day I'll die and have
my revenge on those who have to
read through them.
Miles of chaff.
Pages without end.
You think they don't matter?
Or am I the fool
who thinks they do?

The point is, tonight, I'd fill up
all those pages in an attempt
to stop time with you—
to be with you
and to convey that moment
to you.
Language carries meaning
but it doesn't stop time.
Books stop bullets
but they don't stop time.
This thing I'm feeling for you
is timeless,
yet still it marches madly on.

3.14.2018 aa

You said,
>   I prefer to write by hand
>   and I'm not surprised in the least
>   because you seem like one who would.

You (probably) say,
>   The world need not read my thoughts,
>   I will give it something else
>   to peruse, like photos or drawings
>   or whatever it is that you do.

You said,
>   I'm an adventure with skin on

Well,
you didn't say that
but you'd (probably) agree.
And I'm so tired of wondering
if I'm reading you
like you're reading me.
Or do you have me wrong?
Or do you have me all wrong?
Or is it more fun to
let it unfold and play along?

(Dedicated to the author of the book by Penguin Classics, Well I was
Clearly More Into That Than You Were: A Love Story*)*

The fear, I think,
is that this will become
much more than our kissing
and much more than our fun.

There's something between us,
I think we both see
that it's real as it gets—
it's our ontology.

You're curious and poking
and prodding to know,
and I love that you asked me
if we can go slow.

You're better than good;
you're the freaking best yet,
and it's too soon to tell
if you'll one day say yes.

And so I will not ask,
I'll just start saving up
for a ring and some things
for our merry post-nup.

Come here to me,
let me explain the world:
the way these rocks
squished together like words
in a good poem.
I want to tell you how
it all works,
I want to look into your eyes
I want to read your curiosity,
and feel your heavy sighs.

And you say that you've been
hurt before by someone running fast.
Well I'm a runner baby, but
I hope you won't leave me in the past.

I'm dying to tell you how
the world works,
or how I see it anyway.
I can't promise that it's right,
but oh,
it's all I've got to say.

3/19/2018 as

I remember you—
        at least I think it was you—
walking around a graveyard
on our lunch break.
It was near Andrea's house.
We were too young to ever think
we'd one day join the soil.
No one does until they do,
and only to the worms are they loyal.
I remember us making jokes
and running over tombs
and hopping the fence
to return to our cars.

And now—
        although I'm not sure which one—
you're in a graveyard now.
And you won't eat lunch
or run or laugh or
hop the fence to return to your car.
To the soil, you will be loyal.

A Word to Insecure Men
3/20/2018

Do you ever look at other men
and wonder how they got there?
How'd he get that manly status,
and how come I am not there?
Long have I wondered which ceremony
makes a man a man.
What rite of passage ritual
enables him to stand?
'Cause I feel left out, like there's
something missing from inside.
Some job or skill or confidence
I need to win a bride.

Until I pause and long remember
I'm crafted so uniquely,
and every man who's made a man
has something that he's seeking.
So once for all, I can arrive
being happy being me,
and nevermore wish to exude
another man's identity.

3/25/2018 ae

I think I'm learning how to pace
and how to walk a straighter line—
it's why I never took advantage
of my tons and tons of time.
I'm finally learning how to breathe
and how to trust that you'll be true
just like a compass in my pocket,
I can learn to walk with you.

I think I'm learning to go slower,
to see time with eyes of birds—
to see a friendship start to form between us—
your face I start to learn.
But more than that I'm learning you,
I see your thoughts and how they form.
It's a complex math equation
and it's straying from the norm.

I think I'm learning about boundaries
and how and why they form,
why it isn't always better
to keep tugging till you're torn.
You see, you're wiser than you know
and you have peered right into me—
you told me that you meant it
that you're not a mystery.

Now Let Me Find a Stopping Place
3/26/2018

Now let me find a stopping place
because I've gone and run ahead.
Now let me back myself up here
because this love is nearly dead.

I thought I's doing you a favor,
thought you would appreciate
a hastier departure, but what
you needed was to wait.

Now let me find a stopping place,
I think that I may need your help
to pull the reins up on this horse here,
to put a pause upon our shelf.

Just help me find a stopping point
by saying when and how and where,
because I know that you confuse me,
but that's a burden I can bear.

And now I think I've found a stopping place,
the spot where I can live and breathe.
It wasn't pretty but I made it
and I'm sure you'll be relieved.

4/7/2018 ac

I killed a spider for existing;
he was intruding on my space.
I'm such an enemy of living,
although I've tried to change my ways.

I don't know who or where you are now,
but I will keep you for myself.
I'm just an old unquiet barn owl.
Don't mistake me for someone else.

You turned me in for someone younger
although I rarely act my age.
I thought by now that I'd be stronger,
that I'd be keeping up the pace.

But I'm as fragile as a season,
I see them come and go with ease.
I tried to conjure up a reason
for why you've broken both my knees.

So here I'll stay beside my spider,
with all his curled and busted legs.
I thought by now this fear'd be lighter,
that death would number all my days

but I'm a-slowly getting older
it isn't easy on my bones
and some day soon I'll double over,
and I'll take my spider home.

5/3/2018 ac

This room is new to me,
foreign like a hotel
but lived-in like a home.
Someone else has experienced it
for a substantial segment of life.

Today I decided I don't want
to theorize you.
I don't want to cook up
what life with you would be like.
Let me weigh the pros and cons
of the you I've imagined.

No,
I'd rather experience you.
I'd rather experience life with you,
living in you like a home,
letting life happen within your walls.
And will you stand the test of time?
Will our foundation prove
sturdy enough to bear the weight
of our experiences?

Only more tests can say for sure.
Come, let us experience one another.

I fear who you'll stand next to
and who'll be standing next to her.
But I'm sitting in a stillness
and it's easing my concern.

Yesterday I decided
to relinquish all my guessing.
I'm trying to experience you,
my head is still just stressing.

I think I see from every angle,
I think I've got you figured out.
I think I know you really well
although we never have hung out.

I'm ready to stop thinking,
I'll hit the switch and turn it off
but my brain is hard to downshift
when I don't know you enough.

I see your pixels on the screen and
see you smiling in Brazil
but are you large enough to handle
the giant void you need to fill?

But now I've gone and gave you weight
you know you're never s'posed to have,
so why don't we go out sometime
and we'll just talk and have a laugh.

5/8/2018 aa

You never feel old.
You never feel mature.
Life is a run-on sentence and you
only realize it
when you don't sleep for a night.
Time doesn't stop;
it is not punctuated by pauses or

rests.

You never get to catch your
breath.

Today I see you sitting on the
rail of our favorite dock and
it feels like another lifetime.
(What did you say to me?
I can't hear you over the last ten years.)
It's not,
it's this one: unbroken and continual.
There has been no divide between that gray
day we sat beside the bay, you
wrapped in my arms
wrapped in that blanket,
and now.

I felt weak and I still do.

I'm becoming suspicious that
we never really arrive.
I've just never felt this young before.

Re: That rainy day on Cape Cod in the summer of 2012
5/19/2018

I cried in the coffee shop.
That day was more pure than
the rain.
I wept in the coffee shop
then drove a punch bug all over Cape Cod.
That morning I did a tearful
uncurling of my fists—
a yielding of my desires.

All I wanted was a girl.

Now all I want is to be
back there again,
the purity of that moment—
yes, that one, not this one—
for who travels through time
and emerges with a
moment held in their palm?
I cried in the coffee shop
and then time moved on.

The wise man is he who
is aware of how large a collection
of moments
he has learned from
he has.

5/19/2018
(Right after the previous poem was written.)

All the words I'm trying to
get out
don't fit right on the page—
they hit the paper wrong.
I closed my eyes
and tried to write
but my pen found its way
back to the summer of 2012.

I'm a crook in the wrong house,
I think I was born in
the wrong year.
You're a tornado in a white blouse,
I'm afraid you've got me
all wrong, dear.

CONCLUSION /ABOUT ETHAN

I didn't know if I should put "About the Author," or "About the Poet," or some other descriptive title for the guy who just coughed up this book. Because what the heck is this book? So I went with Ethan, me.

I'm a youth pastor, student and writer. I graduated from Moody Bible Institute in 2015 and started at Denver Seminary in 2017, pursuing the Master of Divinity, emphasis in Theology. Though for right now, the plan is to press pause on school for a moment to go to South America and teach English. The travel itch has arisen again and is begging me scratch. If you read this book attentively, you'll note that I haven't left America since 2012, despite seeing 6/7 continents before the age of 21!

Who knows where we're going, but maybe someday we'll find a stopping place. I wouldn't mind ending up in a place similar to C.S. Lewis' "high country" where the aches of these bones evaporate and we joyfully spring from place to place, more real than the break of day. More real than we've ever realized here on earth.

Well, thanks for putting up with me the past ten years. I still can't tell if this book was just for me, or if you'll get anything out of it too. I hope so. I hope that at the very least, you've felt a sense of camaraderie. Or if I was really good, that I gave some language to some of the thoughts or feelings you've had too. Isn't that what poetry is: Simply an entity which skirts the very boundaries of human language? Maybe it's the language of emotion, or the language of experience.

I feel a little better now.

Thanks for letting me get this book off my chest,

e

Read more at ethanrenoe.com

Made in the USA
Lexington, KY
29 June 2018